Praise for

'Reshma's story of suffering
triumph of the human spirit
remarkable determination t
powerful movement for chan
– **Sir Richard Branson**, businessm..., ..., ,
of Virgin Group

'The story of a survivor, a fighter ... a wake-up call: to fix the
abysmal state of medical care in India, and the deeply entrenched
insensitivity, of hospitals, and even of celebrated doctors'
– **Kavita Krishnan**, women's rights activist and Secretary of the All India
Progressive Women's Association

'*Being Reshma* is a spellbinding read that offers a haunting and
heartwarming look at the life of a young woman who is embroiled
in passions not of her own making, resulting in betrayal and tragedy
that reveals the worst and the best of human nature. If you are only
going to read one book, make this book that one book'
– **Jean Sasson**, international bestselling author of *Princess: A True Story of
Life Behind the Veil of Saudi Arabia* and thirteen other books

'A powerful memoir. Tragic, haunting and inspiring'
– **Keshav Suri**, hotelier and founder of the Keshav Suri Foundation

'This memoir of an incredible young woman's emergence from
the depths of despair is one that will inspire anyone who reads
it. Reshma Qureshi's strength and determination to reclaim her
life, and in doing so, to become a global beacon of hope is truly
inspirational. This powerful memoir is a first-hand account of
surviving a horrific acid attack and provides a rare insight into
the life of one such survivor'
– **John Swinney**, Deputy First Minister of Scotland and Cabinet Secretary
for Education and Skills

'Reshma's story is a must-read for everyone. Fighting back after a
brutal, cowardly acid attack and walking the ramp at international
fashion shows is a strong statement against female oppression.
There is much to learn from her inspirational life'
– **Sachin Tendulkar**, internationally renowned cricketer and former captain
of the Indian cricket team

Praise for Being Reshma

'*Being Reshma* is a powerful story of courage, perseverance and triumph. This crisp yet emotionally grounded narrative not only enables the reader to connect with acid-attack victim Reshma, but also brings to life the reality of violence and humiliation that many women in India continue to face. A significant achievement and a compelling read'

– **Shashi Tharoor**, Indian politician, Member of Parliament and bestselling author

'An inspiration; truly championing the cause of women's empowerment'

– **Asmita Arya**, *Scoop Whoop*/scoopwhoop.com

'*Being Reshma* isn't only an account of an acid-attack survivor's harrowing road to recovery, it is also about the fight against any and all kinds of oppression'

– **Indrani Bose**, *Financial Express*

'Recounted in smooth, swift prose … *Being Reshma* is a vital read to get some perspective on privilege and people who actually live difficult lives'

– **Sneha Bhura**, *Week*

'An immensely moving memoir … *Being Reshma* is a rallying cry for change'

– **Rupert Hawksley**, *National*

'A story of resilience … It's hard not to be moved by this young woman's courage'

– **R. Krithika**, *Hindu*

'Heart-wrenching. Tragic. Miraculous. Extraordinary'

– **Anushree Tiwari Sharma**, *Free Press Journal*

'In *Being Reshma*, acid-attack survivor Reshma Qureshi gives us an immensely moving memoir that exposes the depths of human depravity, while simultaneously offering a glimmer of hope'

– **Piyusha Vir**, *Women's Web*/womensweb.in

Being Reshma

Reshma Qureshi is an Indian model, vlogger and anti-acid-sale activist. She is the face of Make Love Not Scars, an NGO that works towards rehabilitating and empowering acid-attack survivors.

Tania Singh is the CEO of Make Love Not Scars. She lives in New Delhi.

Being Reshma

The Extraordinary Story
of an Acid-Attack Survivor
Who Took the World by Storm

RESHMA QURESHI

with

TANIA SINGH

PAN

First published in hardcover 2018 by Macmillan
This edition first published 2019 by Pan
an imprint of Pan Macmillan Publishing India Private Limited
707, Kailash Building,
26, K. G. Marg, New Delhi – 110 001
www.panmacmillan.co.in

Pan Macmillan, 20 New Wharf Road, London N1 9RR
Basingstoke and Oxford
Associated companies throughout the world
www.panmacmillan.com

ISBN 978-93-89109-08-5

Typeset in Sabon LT Std by R. Ajith Kumar, New Delhi
Printed and bound in India by
Gopsons Papers Ltd.

To Make Love Not Scars, an organization like no other, with all my love and gratitude

Contents

CONTENTS

Foreword

WHEN I WAS ASKED to write this foreword, I put it off for over six months. I was terrified of doing injustice to two of the most important people in my life.

I remember the first time I met Reshma like it was just yesterday. I truly believe that life has this way of making you meet certain people for very specific reasons. By the time we met, Reshma hadn't spoken for days and had undergone a couple of medical procedures. Make Love Not Scars had already fundraised for her treatment by then so she had heard about my existence. I don't think she knew then that I wasn't much older than her. The day we met, I like to think that she had found comfort in relatability, the same relatability that compelled me to take up Reshma's case.

Back then she was seventeen and I was twenty-one. She had just lived through the most horrific ordeal, but her journey of survival was just beginning. The next few months were hard and included difficult, depressing conversations, moments of silence and a string of sleepless nights. Through these trying times, I would often question the purpose of a life. I would often ask myself how bad things could happen to such good people.

It took a full year for things to start looking up for Reshma. It took a whole year for her to realize the power she possessed because when Reshma finally did start talking again, people actually started listening. Soon, Reshma had become a leading activist in the movement against acid attacks. What Reshma has achieved is no normal feat; her life truly captures the strength and power of the human spirit. This book, the extraordinary story of her life, will haunt, move, inspire and change you.

I had the magical good fortune of meeting Tania Singh, the other most important person in my life, when she volunteered for Make Love Not Scars one day in 2016. It was a busy day, but Tania didn't ask any questions – she was just there to help. While I was taking a break mid-shoot, I had a conversation with her, which would go on to change the future of my organization. This conversation was nothing to write home about, but it laid the foundation for a lifelong friendship. The next day I had my teammate offer

Tania a full-time role, even though she hadn't come to us looking for a job. Tania came into my organization with a former business background and contributed greatly towards developing and refining the existing procedures. Before we knew it, Tania and I had become thick as thieves and have been inspiring and supporting each other since, through good times and bad. I truly cannot remember running Make Love Not Scars without her because she has been so instrumental in making the organization what it is today.

A few months into working with us, Tania had to move to Malaysia to take up a job to which she had previously committed. We watched her go with heavy hearts, but I knew that I had to let her follow her dreams. But it turns out she had moved bag and baggage but left her heart at Make Love Not Scars, because exactly six months into her job I received a call from her asking if she could come back. It turns out my dream was her dream too. Words aren't enough to describe her contribution to our community. Today, Tania is the CEO of Make Love Not Scars and the fact that you have this book in your hands now also makes her an author, a dream she had since she was a child.

Reshma's story, put into words with Tania's tireless help, is an unforgettable one, this book is a labour of great love and friendship. I can only hope it will move you as much as it moved me, and inspires you to take notice of the injustices around us and make a difference.

I can't help but be overwhelmed and moved to tears as I write this foreword, as it means this book is now real, and Reshma's story is now out in the world for everyone to read. This is no longer just a pipe dream on our bucket lists. This is *Being Reshma*.

New Delhi   **Ria Sharma**
September 2018   Founder, Make Love Not Scars

1

Childhood Days

'MEENA, STOP THAT,' I demanded in frustration. I couldn't wait to see when she would outgrow her troublesome, wild streak. She was infamous for her fits of rage and mad, reckless adventures. Her poor misguided father called Meena his little tigress when he would hear of her exploits. Her mother is my age. Just twenty-one. She called Meena a monster when her father wasn't around. At times, she expressed her ardent wish to smack this behaviour out of her far-too-loved and spoilt child. If this is what having children is like, I'm glad I'm still unmarried and childless.

It had only been one hour and I was already tired of her daughter. I stepped in between the two children, attempting to untangle Meena's brother from her clutches. They were my neighbour's children, Ali and

Meena, and I was watching over them. Meena had Ali clutched in a tight grip, his hair clenched in her right fist, while her left arm wrangled his neck with a ferocity that was almost disturbing to witness in a young child. If her left arm was so strong, I feared her dominant one. I managed to free Ali and the poor boy burst into tears. Fair enough – his younger sister had almost ripped half his scalp off.

Aizaz, or Bhai, as we, his three sisters, affectionately call him, began to laugh right after I had diffused the situation by bribing the children with candy. 'How times have changed,' he said. He was right. Nargis, Gulshan, and I had never even dared to raise our voices around our elder brothers, let alone attempt to strangle them. Grabbing them in a headlock would have been a self-inflicted death sentence, or so we were led to believe. Today, our family is different. We fight, argue, and love as equals, but things weren't the same while we were growing up. The word 'bhai' in itself laid out a hierarchy within the siblings.

Being the youngest child in the family, the age difference between my oldest brother Riyaz and me is around twelve years. By the time I had turned five, he was driving a taxi for a living. It was almost like having a third parent. Disrespecting our brothers was an unspoken sin. If anything happened to our father, our brothers would be the ones to earn for Ammi and us girls, arrange our marriages, and ensure that we were taken care of. Ammi made sure that we understood the heavy responsibilities our brothers and father had to bear for our well-being; hence, their happiness came foremost and our part was to keep them happy by behaving well. Grabbing a fistful of their hair would mean a *kadak thappad* from Ammi, no candy for a month, or worse.

Abba, however, was the most respected. So much so that our respect was tinged with an element of fear while growing up. My father was a taxi driver, who owned his own little empire. Well, we joked that he did, but in reality it was just two yellow taxis. Abba had employed another driver on payroll for the cab he didn't drive. When we were younger, we would imagine that our father was a crorepati and make long lists of what we would do with all that money had he actually been one. I would dream of travelling abroad.

One of Abba's friends used to work in Dubai and would bring us the most beautiful foreign toys and chocolates. While we dreamt of being rich, Abba's dream was for his two sons to have real, respectable white-collar jobs, and his three daughters to be happily married and well settled and not have to worry about money. He wanted us to get educated in order for us to find well-educated, respectable husbands.

My eldest brother Riyaz followed in Abba's footsteps

and became a taxi driver himself. However, living in a one-bedroom home with four younger siblings and two parents had left him with an inherent thirst for freedom. This thirst took him on very long drives; he would be out on the road for weeks on end, always returning with exotic sweets from Karnataka, statuettes from Agra, and big, sturdy coconuts from Coimbatore. I now know that Riyaz's decision to not apply for college and follow in Abba's footsteps was a disappointment to both my parents. Abba had placed all his faith in his eldest child, and to watch his son follow his dead-end path almost broke his heart. Luckily, Abba still had Aizaz to test his dreams on.

I grew up in a room on the second floor of a two-storeyed chawl in East Chembur, Mumbai. In a single room that was our whole world, we would awake to the loud voices of our neighbours as they stood in the barely five-foot-wide alley and strained their necks, looking up our staircase towards our closed door. They would scream my mother's name with some demand or the other until they received a satisfactory response. The alley was so dark that, while standing there, it was hard to determine the time of the day.

I realized that the louder voices suggested a stronger relationship between the interlocutors. We were all crude like that. Manners were reserved for those around whom we did not feel comfortable enough. Too much politeness was unsettling, indicating that it was unlikely the acquaintance in question would become a friend. *'Aunty, bachchon ko school le jaogey kya?* Feed them too, we're running late,' was a common demand from working women whose husbands were dead, gone, or bedridden alcoholics. My mother would laugh and invite the kids in, telling them to wait while her own children got dressed.

Riyaz, being the oldest and already working as a driver, no longer went to school. Aizaz, next to Riyaz in the line of siblings, was two years older to our eldest sister, Nargis. Aizaz, who must have been around twelve when I started going to school at the age of four, would wait patiently for Gulshan, Nargis and me to get dressed and would then walk us and the other children to school.

While navigating the dark, narrow lanes out of our chawl, the smell of permanent dampness shadowed our attempts at deciphering the weather. We knew what the possibility of rain smelt like, but the moisture-laden lanes didn't allow us to put our weatherman skills to use. We always carried umbrellas, just in case. Many of the children suffered more throat aches than they should have. The buildings – if one can call the decrepit structures that – were deformed and weak. To date, we don't know whether the space we occupy is built on lawful ground and no one has ever felt the need to seek professional advice before constructing an extra floor. The families expanded fast; incomes, not so much. The unwieldy top floors of these buildings would merge into each other, blocking out any light. In the evenings, Aizaz would guide us through these treacherous, dark streets with a torch.

We called him the Pied Piper of Chembur. While Nargis, Gulshan and I were deeply respectful of our brother, the neighbours' children were wild ragamuffins. They would stop along the way to buy sweets or chase cats or try to convince my brother to look the other way while they conferred about skipping school. Aizaz would hover over them, scorn etched across his face, and just as he would threaten to call their parents the kids would all fall into a spectacular single line and follow him straight to school. The girls and boys attended different schools. The girls would be dropped off first and Aizaz would then lead the boys to their school.

I would walk back alone from school since my classes would finish earlier than those of the older children. One day, when I was around six, I had my first terrible day at school. My friend Amira and I got into trouble for laughing at the teacher while she was scolding us for not doing our homework. We were both made to sit apart from each other for the rest of the day and given additioinal mathematics homework. I had to spell the numbers one through hundred in capital letters. I thought that was far too much homework for a six-year-old. To cheer myself up, I decided to buy orange candy on my way home. They were these heavenly little sugar balls glazed with artificial colouring. I would suck on them until my tongue went numb. These orange candies were a staple of my childhood, and to date I feel a sense of satisfaction when I see children reaching for Parle orange candy at the local cigarette store. Some things never go out of fashion, I guess.

That day I sucked on the candy while walking back from school, skipping and humming happily as I held on to both straps of my backpack to spread out the weight of the books that were strapped on my back. I estimate that the books must have been about a quarter of my weight. Our schools didn't have any lockers.

As I ran down the alley, I jumped over every pothole that I had memorized into my footwork. During the monsoons, these potholes would disappear under the water flowing through our streets. Our mother had forced us to commit these potholes to memory to ensure we never fell into them. Whenever she read in the papers of an untimely death by falling into a pothole, she would make us jog our memories, just for her peace of mind.

I continued sucking on the orange candy, cursing my class teacher, and jumping over these very potholes when I heard a man walking down the alley, whistling as he came closer. '*Biscuits, namkeen, samosey, garam garam pakorey*,' he kept repeating in a singsong voice. As he came even closer, his voice became even more melodious. '*Biscuits, namkeen, samosey, garam garam pakorey*.' And his offerings seemed even more tempting. I suddenly realized how hungry I was. I looked into my pockets for some change, but found none. I had spent it all on a ridiculous amount of orange candy.

'*Bhaiya, Bhaiya*,' I stopped him in his tracks. '*Mujhe na ek packet biscuit dena*,' I said, after momentarily weighing my options. I knew we had samosas at home, namkeen didn't sound appealing, and street vendors always sold stale pakoras. I knew I had to have a packet of biscuits. I chose the elaichi biscuits, my favourite. 'Five rupees,' he said, as he handed me a packet of sweet cardamom biscuits that always tasted like a mix of the spice, sugar, honey, and salt. I looked down at my feet, mumbling a pitiful request for him to follow me to my house since I had no money and was sure that Ammi would have some.

'I don't have time for that,' he said gruffly, as he

put out his hands and asked me to return the packet. I really, really wanted the biscuits and tried to sneak a peek at the gutter on my right. Sometimes, my friends and I would hunt for coins in the open drains, often to our luck. That day, however, my eyes could pick up not even a hint of shiny metal.

Just when I was about to lose hope and hand over the biscuits, I was struck by what seemed like a brilliant idea. 'Wait, bhaiya,' I said as I bent down and fiddled with my ankle. 'Take this in exchange for the biscuits,' I said as I handed him my anklet. I secretly prayed that the man would accept my anklet instead of the five rupees because he seemed confused by my bargaining skills. His face was clouded with doubt for a moment, but he broke into a smile and accepted the piece of jewellery. 'Here, beta,' he said as he pulled out an extra packet of biscuits and handed it to me. 'Take this too.'

Extremely proud of my conquest, I finished both packets of biscuits and rushed home to brag about my victory to whoever was available. I made sure to carry the empty packets as proof. My siblings had a tendency to brush off my adventures as figments of an over-imaginative mind.

Gulshan reached home around the same time as me. I offered her some candy and began to tell her about my day. She laughed hysterically at my adventures until I started telling her about my hunt for coins on the streets. The minute she heard about my final exchange her face went sullen. 'What were you thinking, you silly girl?' she said as she grabbed me by my arms and shook me. I was stunned, wondering what I had done wrong. 'Calm down,' I said in irritation and stood up defiantly. 'What's your problem? Are you upset that I didn't get you any biscuits?' I asked.

'No, you fool. Your anklet was made of gold. Real gold! Do you have any idea how expensive that is?'

I felt my heart start to race and my hands get clammy. I did not know exactly how much gold cost, but I knew for us it was a fortune. I had heard women talk about how they scrounged, put away, and hid money from their husbands to save for gold for their daughters' weddings. One woman's daughter had even committed suicide when her wedding was called off because the man she loved was not pleased with the gold he had been given.

I panicked as my mind raced for a solution. I could run back and try to find the man or perhaps I could sell my books. It's not as though I liked studying. I could maybe get a job. While I came up with a list of possible solutions, Gulshan had already recounted the incident to my mother. That is the first memory I have of my mother slapping me. It wasn't violent or painful, but it is forever etched in my mind because of what happened later that very same day.

That night my father returned home to learn over dinner the havoc I had caused. This was the first time in the six years of my life that my father had had to hear a complaint about me. Normally he would unleash his wrath upon my brothers and often I had trembled at the thought of having the same anger come down on me. As Ammi and Gulshan continued to tell him about my pathetic bargaining skills, I began to feel heavily the fear trapped in my chest. My knees began to tremble and I clasped my two hands behind my back, expecting the worst.

'Look at what she did,' said Ammi, as she pointed at me. 'She will be the death of me. Do you know how many things I denied myself to be able to buy her that anklet?'

'Abba,' I said crying, and my nose started to drip clumsily. 'Abba, I'm so sorry. I promise I will work and pay you back and I will never eat candy again. Why did you even give me a gold anklet? Who gives a six-year-old real gold? And why didn't you tell me it was expensive? How would I know what gold is?' I truly believed that laying the blame on my parents' decision-making skills would help me get off easier.

At first he was stunned. And then, to everyone's surprise and dismay, he began to laugh. 'You must have as many biscuits as you want. We wouldn't want the neighbours to think that we starve our children.

From tomorrow give Reshma five rupees for biscuits every day.' He smiled and put some more food on my plate. 'Eat, you skinny little girl,' he said as he got up from the *chattai* to put his plate in the sink and left me to finish my meal at my own, slow pace. Once I was done and everyone had stopped commenting on my father's uncharacteristic response, we sat down to have tea. 'Reshma, I wouldn't expect anything less from you,' said Abba as he began to laugh. 'Do you know about the day you were born? That was the day I first knew you would be a troublesome little rabbit for the rest of your life.'

I shook my head, egging him on to tell me more about the day I was born. My entire family burst out with charged anecdotes about the exact day they first discovered that life would never be the same again. This had partly to do with the circumstances surrounding my birth.

The supposed beginning of this great adventure known as my life was marked with two of my mother's plans being ungraciously put to an end. First, I wasn't born as per her well-organized plans, and second, she never ended up buying the fish she had so painstakingly argued over.

I listened to several versions of the events from Abba, Ammi, Riyaz, and Aizaz. Gulshan and Nargis were still relatively young when I was born, however,

Nargis' description of the events surrounding my birth was the most compelling of all.

Apparently, October 1996 had graced the city with calm as the torrential rains grew tired and the unforgiving Mumbai monsoon came to a long-awaited halt. A climatologically undefined season – a pendulum between monsoon and post-monsoon – barraged our city with hot days and cool nights.

My mother was too much of a pessimist to not take advantage of the predictable weather. Life had taught her to be on her guard, even when things seemed somewhat stable. The systematic transition of hot days to cool nights wouldn't last for long and she feared the sludge of the Mumbai gutters gushing through our alleys. At all costs she wanted to avoid being outdoors when the rain returned.

My mother pieced together an impenetrable argument for her elder sister, Salma. The facts were simple. The rains had come to a stop after a long time and my mother had less than two weeks to go before her due date. As Salma was well aware, no matter what happened, our home had to keep running and the fish had to be bought and frozen. After all, there were four other children to be fed along with a husband. There was no convincing my mother otherwise, and Salma Maasi sighed and heaved and pretended to make a huge fuss, but eventually gave in to my pregnant mother's demands and accompanied her to the Koliwada fish mandi in Chembur (East).

Shopping at a local Mumbai fish market is a challenging exercise for the city's sheltered and wealthy locals. But for us it is an extension of our daily lives. Upon entering the market, we are assaulted by an unruly mix of sights and sounds. The blazing sun burns our heads. As children, we used to compete amongst ourselves by touching each other's heads to see which one was the hottest. For some reason one of the girls always won.

It is best recommended to wear a pair of rubber slippers, something cheap yet of lasting quality, like a pair of hand-me-down Bata. The streets flow with liquid grime, as the large blocks of ice attempting to preserve the freshness of the variety of local and foreign fish melt and fuse with the dirt on the narrow paths. Returning home would always entail a rigorous session of cleaning one's feet as well as footwear.

On the morning of 13 October 1996, my mother and maasi were busy examining the chimbori, basa, pomfret, and, a rare Bengali favourite, the bhetki. It was a clammy day; the air was laden with the kind of humidity that turns clothes into magnets. Their clothes clinged to their bodies like cellophane wrap. My mother had reached the mandi early, hoping to avoid the crowds. However, no matter how early one reached, the mandi was always swarming with people. Fisherwomen, with saris tightly tucked into petticoats that strangled their waists and accentuated rolls of belly fat, would walk by, shouting, 'Side please, side please, side please,' carrying on their heads large bamboo baskets containing the catch of the day.

My mother would always wonder about the fisherwomen's struggles to raise children on their own. Back in the day, women didn't really work, and if they did it was probably because they had fallen on desperate times. Things have not changed all that much since.

The fisherwomen would hustle to find a spot to set up shop and if they had a meagre catch, they would gravitate like ants towards the other women of similar destiny; they would all then set up stalls together. People would walk past in human chains, pushing and shoving against one another. Families would link arms and walk in the mandi, just in case one got lost.

This exhausting environment should have been enough to deter a pregnant woman from entering the fish mandi, but my mother was not like most women. While many would not come to shop early in the morning, my mother was often the first to reach.

The first sale of the morning is considered auspicious by most shopkeepers in India. During this period of *bauni*, attempts at bargaining can be compared to throwing a hammer on one's own foot. Many consider shopping during the bauni period to be self-destructive since shopkeepers try a variety of tactics to make the first shopper of the day pay more than the fair price. Reasons cited range from 'My whole day's business depends on this sale' to 'God will grant you good luck and health' and even 'Karma will give you the healthiest fish of the lot'. We Indians pride ourselves on being pragmatic with money, yet tremble with fear when it comes to opposing superstitious beliefs. At the end of the day, very few have the courage to bargain during the period of bauni and my mother was one of those zealots.

My mother was pressed to the fish cart as sellers kept pushing and shoving in an attempt to pass through and set up for the day. But my mother stood her ground and picked up a plastic bag as she examined different sizes of pomfret. 'Ma, that'll be a hundred and fifty,' said the fisherwoman.

'Too much,' said my mother with an exasperated sigh as she dropped the fish and picked up another. The fisherwoman pulled out a large knife and indicated the quantity she could sell for less. 'This much, hundred only,' she said.

'Eighty,' said my mother as she picked up the piece and put it in her plastic bag.

'No, Ma. How?' said the fisherwoman as she tried the age-old classic Indian sales pitch inspired by the concept of guilt-tripping the buyer. 'I might as well give it to you for free. A present from a poor fisherwoman.'

'No, no. How could I?' responded my mother with a big smile. 'I will just have to go to another stall.'

'But ... but,' the fisherwoman stuttered. 'This is bad for my bauni. My entire day's sales will be ruined.'

As the argument continued, I decided that the best way to put an end to it would be to announce my arrival at what my mother says was the most inopportune moment. Just as she was about to convince the fisherwoman to sell her the pomfret at the right price, my mother stopped mid-sentence to clench my maasi's arm. 'Salma,' she said, calmly. 'Take me to the hospital.'

My mother had gone into labour and Maasi quickly pushed through the crowd and flagged down an auto. The auto driver drove like a maniac to Chanda Hospital in Chembur. And that is how I was born on 13 October 1996 in a tiny hospital room.

My misadventure forgotten in light of re-living fond family memories, we laid prepared to go to sleep once all my childish questions had been answered. That was a happy night, one that I remember even today. That night, just like every other night, we all laid out our colourful jute mats to sleep on the cement floor, right next to one another. I complained about how thin the mat was and, as usual, Ammi said that the thinner the mattress, the better it was for my back. She groaned as she placed her gnarled fingers on the floor for support and bent over to kiss my forehead. 'I love you, beta. Anyone can make a mistake,' she whispered into my ear just as I was about to doze off. I caught a whiff of the lavender oil she was used to dabbing on her wrists. I was never sent to bed without being told just how much my mother loved me. Mumbai changed, my family changed, I changed. But some things always stayed the same.

2

Ammi

'DO YOU REMEMBER HOW you would try to pronounce Ammi's name when you were a kid?' said Gulshan, as I sat crying on the floor, refusing to eat my breakfast and demanding to know where Ammi was. I was missing my mother. In my alley everyone has a heartbreaking fondness for memories. In our world, where the future is considered to be as grim as the past (if not grimmer), we obsessively linger over the happy days. Gulshan asked me if I remembered my carefully constructed tomboy outfits or the numerous glass toys my eldest brother brought back from his travels. She tried to pull a few out, but I ignored her efforts at cheering me up through these feeble distractions. Glass horses and cats for a six-year-old – an unprecedented luxury in my neighbourhood. Dangerous too, but no one worries about that because there's more danger where the toys came from. There once was a toy-seller who raped a girl who hadn't even turned thirteen. He was tied to a pole and beaten up till the cops arrived. Gulshan didn't need to remind me of that part of the story. My mother had etched it into my mind, along with a fear of unknown men.

Ammi's birth name is Khakhanuma. Not exactly easy on a child's tongue. I used to call her Kakha. On that particular morning I was crying because it must have been something like the third day in a row that Ammi had left home before I had even woken up. I was eight and I can't exactly remember how many days it had been, but it was enough to make me break down. My sisters, Gulshan and Nargis, who were by then twelve and fourteen respectively, got me ready for school and prepared to send me off. But I wouldn't stop crying. Nargis handed me my water bottle and tiffin box, while Gulshan carried my schoolbag and gently nudged me out of the door. She carried my bag all the way to school. Now that Aizaz was in the tenth standard, his day would begin earlier. He also had early-morning private tuitions for his board exams.

Gulshan and I reached school and I met my friend Amira at the gate. The minute I saw her I forgot about my distress and began to gossip about the latest rumour that was spreading across our school. Jamina, a senior, had stopped coming to school recently. We heard that she had been married off. She was thirteen. 'Stop talking about things you know nothing of, you chattermouths,' said Gulshan, and gave me a slight whack on my head. 'Wait till you hear people talking shit about you one day.'

Amira and I giggled as we walked into the school building hand in hand. I forgot to ask Gulshan why Nargis and she weren't coming to school nowadays. I hated school, preferring to play outdoors rather than be stuck inside. Once I realized that no matter what mistakes I made I would get away with it, I began pushing the limits. I would skip class to go play in the rain, pretend I'd submitted my homework and blame the teacher for losing my notebook when she asked for me to turn it in, and often talked loudly while class was on, in order to get kicked out. But while I pushed the limits, the limits sometimes ended up pushing me right back. It was on this particular day that I realized my actions were catching up with me and that things were changing. I had to now start becoming more responsible, because my family was struggling with certain insurmountable changes.

After school ended that day I decided to go and play with some friends. It was sometime in March 2003 and the weather was good for a change. We played hide-and-seek and hopscotch, and I forgot to inform Gulshan or Nargis that I'd be out late. When I reached home at around five or six in the evening I found Gulshan, Nargis, and Aizaz waiting for me, worried. As usual, Riyaz, Abba, and Ammi weren't home. I walked in, nonchalantly singing the latest Bollywood songs, not noticing the worried looks on their faces.

'Where were you? You are supposed to come straight home from school,' screeched Gulshan, as she grabbed me by my arms, shaking me like a rag doll. 'Stop that,' I screamed as I pushed her away.

'Don't you dare talk to your sister like that, you spoilt, rotten child. We were just about to call Riyaz. Do you know how worried Ammi and Abba would have been?' said Aizaz. Gulshan added her two paise: 'Go wash up. You look filthy.'

'You're not Ammi and you have no right to tell me what to do. Nargis and you haven't even been to school this last week. I won't go either if you continue to act like such witches,' I screamed back in anger. I flung my school bag on the floor right next to Gulshan's feet.

Taken aback, Gulshan burst into tears, and so did I. Gulshan, Nargis and I had been friends for as long as I could remember. I had never had to take orders from them. The last few days, however, had seen a change in our relationship. They had been sending me to school and even following up on my homework. They had been cooking our meals and ordering me around. I

22

couldn't bear the hypocrisy. It was as though Ammi had disappeared, and Gulshan and Nargis had taken her place without a second thought or an explanation to me. The fact that I had to carry on with my life as if things were normal had finally taken a toll on me. The way Gulshan and Nargis had taken over Ammi's role seemed to me like a betrayal to Ammi. How could life be so normal when she wasn't around? Things should have changed. Our routines should not have been as consistent as they were. Moreover, I hated my sisters – how easily they felt they could replace Ammi. Plus, it's not like they were much older than I was.

Aizaz calmed us all down. 'Look, Reshma. Ammi, Abba and Riyaz are out on some important work, but Ammi will be back soon. She'll be very upset to see you this thin and scrawny and we'll all get into trouble for starving you. Until then, why don't you help your sisters? Look how nicely they've been taking care of you. Why don't you wipe those tears off? You're probably hungry. Have you eaten lunch? Gulshan made you some biryani.'

Aizaz always knew how to cheer me up. Back then, I used to live for biryani. I still do. I quickly went to wash my hands and face and ran off to peer through the curtains that doubled as the door to our makeshift kitchen where my eldest sister Gulshan, still sniffling, was heating some chicken biryani in a steel pan. I remember that pan because it was black grime. On weekends I would sit with a dish exfoliator and lime-infused dish soap, struggling to clean the grime. It was not a bad way to pass the time. Of course, I never succeeded at making the pan shine.

I ate my meal, did my homework, and went off to sleep. Ammi, Abba and Riyaz came home late that night, just like they would every other night. The minute I heard the door open, I became alert. I heard footsteps. I closed my eyes tighter. The door creaked open and I opened my eyes just enough to be able to make out the door. I could make out shapes in the light coming in through a crack in the door. With the assurance that my brother, father and mother were home, I dozed off peacefully.

The next day happened to be a Sunday. I woke up a little later than usual and jumped straight out of bed when I realized that Ammi was home. I ran into her arms and remember feeling terrified that I might hurt her because of how different she seemed. It had only been a few days, but even I could see the clothes hanging on a visibly thinner frame and the limp, lifeless hair that shone with lustre just days ago. 'Ammi, where have you been?' I shouted. Abba gently lifted me out of her lap. 'She's been with us,' he said, without further explanation.

'Yes, but where? What have you been doing?' I prodded.

'Reshma, stop asking questions. Mind your own business, just as a child should,' said Riyaz, putting an end to my pestering. Since Bhai had told me to shut up, I shut up. I didn't even need any answers because I was happy just to have Ammi back.

I sat right next to Ammi and began to build a puzzle, while Gulshan kept reminding me to finish my glass of milk. I remember wishing I had a dog to pass it off to. Soon after, my mother placed her glass of water in the only sink we had in our home and grabbed her bag. Her eyes were swollen and her movements, lethargic. 'I'll see you later, beta,' she said as she skirted past me, towards the door. I turned to see my father and brother standing at the doorway, waiting for her. 'Won't you stay for lunch?' I asked, a lump forming in my throat. There was an unusual lull in the house, a quietness that even to my naive ears whispered a premonition. 'No, Gulshan will feed you,' she said. The door slammed shut.

Over the next few days I sank into a massive cesspit of depression. As an eight-year-old, this intense feeling of sorrow was unlike anything I had ever experienced before. I stopped going to school just like Gulshan and Nargis had, tears poured relentlessly out of my eyes, escaping my notice. No one noticed. I had always been a shy child and it was easy for my sentiments and personality to become intertwined, confused.

I didn't know why my mother disappeared for long periods of time. I just wish someone had told me. Something extraordinarily horrific was happening and I was purposely being kept in the dark. Every time Ammi returned home, her hair seemed dry and ragged, like that of a homeless woman who had not showered for days. I could see broken strands clinging to her *abaaya* and my father supported her now-thinner frame towards the only bed we had. She would enter the house and lie down immediately. She would refuse water, tea and food. She seemed sick and smelled sick.

Soon, Ammi would be gone for days on end. One day, towards the beginning of April, I began to cry miserably. The days of quietly witnessing the steady change in family dynamics had finally taken their toll on me and I was no longer the quiet, understanding child that my family was accustomed to. I refused to go to school, refused to eat, and shed tears through ragged breaths. I was crying so much for my mother that I couldn't even swallow the glasses of water my sisters kept foisting on me. They thought I would faint and Aizaz was sent an urgent summon. Aizaz must have called Abba because soon after my father returned home to be presented with a helpless version of myself.

I heard words being whispered between Gulshan and Abba. 'We can't tell her,' Abba said. 'We must; Nargis is only three years older than her. If she knows, why can't Reshma? Look at her, Abba, it's time to tell her. She's stopped going to school already. She's too young to stop going to school.'

It took some convincing on Gulshan's part, but, at last, Abba sat down next to me and wiped my tears. 'Reshma,' he said, as he gently placed his arm around my shoulders. 'I'm going to tell you something, but only because I think you're a big, brave girl. Are you a big, brave girl?'

I nodded, excited to finally be in on the family secret, but afraid at the same time. I knew something was miserably wrong. 'Beta, Ammi is safe, she is with us. Reshma, please . . . ' he begged me as he got down on his knees and held me by my shoulders. 'Eat your food and I will take you to see Ammi and explain everything.'

I gulped down my meal, jumped into a pair of slippers, and demanded that we leave immediately. My father held my hand as we descended the stairs. He hailed an auto and I wondered why we didn't just take one of his taxis.

In the auto, we sat in silence, the dry heat beating against my face as the driver manoeuvred through the crowded Mumbai streets. My father spoke to me only once. He told me to move towards the middle of the seat and to stay away from the open side. I complied. As we pulled up to our destination I couldn't help but notice the hundreds of people sleeping on the streets outside. I looked out of the auto and saw a big red cross. We were at a hospital.

My father paid the auto driver without haggling. He grabbed my hand and told me to stay close. We made our way through throngs of confused people, till we were finally able to get in. Many people were arguing with the guards, attempting to get into an elevator leading to the second floor where the ICU was. My father just pushed through, showed the guard an ID, and we went up. The rest of them were left standing outside, helpless without passes. I was petrified. The hospital smelt just like my mother's skin every time I hugged her and it made me want to cry all over again.

I couldn't, though; my father was moving too fast and I was almost running to match my stride with his. If I had a moment, just a moment, I know I would have broken down. We reached a large doorway with another guard posted outside. 'No children,' he said, the minute he saw us walking up. My father remained quiet.

'Sir, please,' he said. 'Her mother is in there and my daughter is scared. She needs to see her mother.'

'Why? Is she dying?' he asked, without a care. 'No children,' repeated the guard when he received no response. He continued to chew on his paan and flipped out a phone. 'There are other patients inside and your child will make unnecessary noise.'

This man's insensitivity haunts me even today. Inside, people were fighting to stay alive, and outside, this man was in charge of appeasing their tormented family members. I never understood why he was hired.

'Sir,' my father begged this heartless guard. 'I will not take her inside. Please, allow me to just carry her on my shoulders and she can see her mother through the window.'

If it had been any other situation I would have gently held my father's hand and pulled him away. It hurt me to see him demeaning himself in this manner. However, this one time, I allowed him to beg. I needed to see my mother and was on the verge of begging to the guard myself. At last, I began to cry.

The guard sighed and nodded. He lifted a finger lethargically and pointing us towards the ICU. I knew he agreed more out of annoyance than compassion. He was just too tired to continue arguing.

My father led me towards the ICU. A door opened as a nurse exited, and a blast of cold, damp air hit me, but we didn't go through that door. I was scared. I had never been to an ICU before.

My father lifted me up on his shoulders and I put my hands on his head for support. The memories from the days before and after have now diminished into disjointed fragments. I remember events, many of which have been pieced together by those around me. But the memory of my father holding me up as I peered inside through an oval window on the ICU door is one I will never forget.

The smell of the hospital, the confused people, shattered lives, and the occasional churlish laughter – the fragments fused together form a disturbing picture. However, there is one particular sight that I remember as if it was yesterday. My mother, lying on a bed with the blanket hanging off the side, with tubes down her throat and needles stuck in her arm. She was barely awake and surrounded by misery. Yet, at that moment, I finally knew where my mother had been and felt pure joy, mixed with a hard, cold fear. So much fear. While still on my father's shoulders, peering through the forbidden window, I knew death was a force to be reckoned with. This was my first realization of my mother's mortality.

We returned home in a rickshaw. My mother never knew I had paid her a visit. Had she known, she would have been outraged. I was too young to be in hospitals and was not allowed to see her in that state. At least, that's what she would say with indignation.

As quiet as we had been on our way to the hospital, the return home was just as loud. I couldn't help but ask all the questions to which I knew I would now get answers.

Abba began with an apology. 'Ammi didn't want you to know, beta. She thought you were too young and we didn't want you to worry.'

'Worry about what?' I asked.

Ammi had been diagnosed with stomach cancer. I didn't know what cancer was since I was just eight and this was the first time I had paid attention to the word. My mother had a terrible, poisonous growth in her stomach and my family wanted to protect me from this knowledge. Apparently, Gulshan and Nargis had dropped out of school to manage the house and take care of me. Ammi had been very unwell, but, Alhamdulillah, she had managed to get into surgery that morning itself and the growth had been successfully removed.

'But if she had surgery today, where was she all the other days?' I asked. 'She was getting chemotherapy to shrink the tumour,' Abba replied. I found out she was better now and that Gulshan and Nargis would not be returning to school because Ammi would need assistance for herself as well as with managing the home through the coming few months and we obviously could not afford a full-time nurse.

I discovered answers to questions I didn't even know existed. After getting married, my father worked hard to provide a comfortable life for his family. Little by little he denied himself basic comforts in order to give us more of them. He started working as a driver for an employer in Mumbai for a salary of eight thousand rupees and used his savings to become an independent taxi-owner. Over a span of two decades he had bought two cars and had employed a driver for the car he didn't drive. The day my mother was diagnosed with stomach cancer, he knew what mattered. Keeping her alive.

Abba and Riyaz took her to one of the largest private hospitals in Mumbai. Reference after reference later, they were continuously told that my mother's cancer had advanced beyond hope. She would die. But at last, Abba and Bhaiya found a well-known private hospital that believed surgery would lead to a positive outcome. They demanded five lakh rupees, a fortune for us. Without a second thought my father sold his taxi business: two taxis and his livelihood.

The surgery never took place and the money was never returned. As my mother waited for surgery at the hospital, she was shocked to witness the unhygienic state of affairs. Needles were reused and rarely disposed of, and once when wheeled into the operation theatre she emerged screaming. Inside, the bed she was to use still carried the last patient's blood and the surgical equipment looked rusted. She refused to be operated upon in such conditions and demanded a clean operation theatre or that their money be returned. She wanted the kind of care for which her family had sacrificed everything.

The hospital claimed that she having already entered the operation theatre and refused surgery of her own free will, her funds had already been utilized. It wasn't their fault that she had refused to go through with the surgery; the expenses had already been borne by the hospital. She was refused further treatment and my family was ignored by the hospital. Every time my father tried to go to the finance department, he was told to wait untill the end of the day and then asked to leave because visiting hours were over.

Getting involved with the cops was not an option because the hospital had us convinced that they were well acquainted with the hospital owners. My father had no choice but to forget about the wasted money, the loss of his only source of income, his life's efforts being wasted on a corrupt and bureaucratic system, and, most of all, face the possibility that my mother may not survive because he trusted the wrong establishment.

I tried to act relieved, pretending to myself that my mother was better, but my fears returned when my father started to speak. His hands shook as he kept repeating, 'It's fine, it's fine, everything's fine.' I knew it was more for his benefit than mine. How could everything be fine? This was probably the first time my father had acknowledged our financial ruin out loud, and that too to his eight-year-old daughter sitting at the back of a rickshaw. We reached the lane outside our chawl and walked home quietly. Tea was prepared and he sat down to complete his story.

'We may have lost everything, beta. But we've got Ammi, we've got each other. We've got our home in Mau Aima, Inshallah. We're alright. We're lucky.' My sisters looked scared as they repeated his words. I knew that words could only provide scant comfort, but we had lost our source of income. But the story wasn't over.

'But, Abba,' I asked, 'how did the surgery become possible?'

My father smiled for the first time that day. After the tragic series of events that took place for her surgery, my father was almost penniless and completely hopeless. He stood outside the hospital, crying under a tree, right next to a tea stall. This is when a sad thought crossed his mind: should he buy a cup of tea or save the money? He said he didn't know why, but for some reason he kept looking up at the sky for help. His vision gravitated to where he believed God was. It was as though he had nothing else left to witness. Just then a man walked up to Abba and, placing a hand on his shoulder, asked him why he was crying. He bought my father a cup of tea and began to talk to him. This kind, generous stranger spent an hour listening to his ordeals. 'Bhaijaan,' he said at last. 'Take your wife to Ismailia Hospital.' This stranger handed my father a doctor's number at Ismailia Hospital and never asked for anything in return. We never found out his name.

We found hope again in the help extended by a kind stranger who was moved by a grown man crying under a tree. My father took his advice and convinced Ammi to visit Ismailia Hospital. She had given up on hospitals altogether, but Abba appealed to her love for her children and for Allah. 'Maybe Allah had sent that man to me,' he said.

As it turned out, this other hospital had a charitable foundation, and owing to our financial situation Ammi agreed to the surgery, since the conditions of this hospital were more humane and the doctors far kinder than the ones she had had to deal with at the last hospital. She had her surgery at a miniscule cost at Ismailia Hospital, funded by generous donations. The tumour had been removed at last.

I was the first one, besides Abba and Bhai, to see Ammi at the hospital after her surgery. I never went back to the hospital, but a few days later Ammi returned home and was on bed rest for months. My sisters dropped out of school willingly in order to cook, clean, and take care of my mother and the rest of us, but everyone insisted I carry on with school. My family came together, seared with tragedy, but kindled with love.

Years later I realized that kindness knows no bounds and as violent and cruel India can be, it is also home to the gentlest people on earth. The kind stranger who saved my mother's life is just one of such people I've met over the years.

3

Life in Mau Aima

AMMI STRUGGLED TO RECOVER from the painful effects of eradicating cancer, while my sisters sacrificed their education to care for her. For two years my elder sisters, Gulshan and Nargis, looked after my cancer-stricken mother. To incur the expenses – Ammi's surgeries, chemotherapy, medication, and post-operative doctor visits – my father started working as a driver for a taxi company. The family income had taken a severe hit, and Riyaz and Abba were putting every single rupee into ensuring that the household could run as smoothly as possible. Expenses were cut and I started wearing hand-me-downs. We couldn't afford nurses or domestic help, so my sisters took over the household chores besides looking after my mother.

We lived in Mumbai for over two more years after Ammi's surgery in 2004. Towards the beginning of 2007, when I had just turned ten, we realized that living in Mumbai was simply not going to be affordable any more. Despite the fact that Aizaz had just turned eighteen and given up on his dream of attending university and instead begun working in a small company so he could contribute towards the family's income, we were still struggling to make ends meet. Ammi had recovered by this time and the only fear we had was that of a possible relapse. Abba's parents had a house in Mau Aima, a village in Allahabad. It was decided that Nargis, Gulshan, Ammi and I would move there to reduce the financial burden on my father and brothers. Moreover, village life would be more suitable for Ammi's health.

We moved to Mau Aima in January 2007. The school year ended in March so I joined a new school just in time for the Class Five finals. For a brief period, there was some talk of Gulshan and Nargis resuming school, but the idea was quickly discarded. It had been far too long already since they had dropped out and neither of them was keen in any case to go on to college or look for jobs. What would be the point? Gulshan was fifteen and she would probably be getting married in the next few years. As with many other girls in our community, their education had been cut short because they were too set in their domestic ways.

Moving to Mau Aima in 2007 had its benefits, but wasn't without its share of challenges either. For one, I desperately missed my friends and Mumbai's vibrant energy. When I first arrived to live in Mau Aima, I was surprised by how my family had become the centre of attention. Neighbours would drop by for tea with their children and throw numerous questions our way. 'Is it true that you're from Mumbai?' the children would ask, with wonder in their eyes. 'We've heard that there are malls and cinemas in Mumbai and restaurants are open late. Do you often come across actors too?'

For me, Mumbai was just Mumbai. It was my home and not something to spend hours talking about. But in Mau Aima, Mumbai was an unfulfilled dream for many. Children spoke about how they wanted to move there when they were older and the adults spoke about all the opportunities they could have had if only their families had had the vision of moving to the city at an opportune time. It was odd to hear about Mumbai from another's perspective. I guess it's true what they say. One doesn't know the value of what they have until it's lost.

Here, the village children had more rules than we did while growing up in Mumbai. My grandparents had a brick house, a *kachcha ghar*, which was, in essence, incomplete. There was no electricity, and at night we would have to light candles. The red bricks of the walls were stacked together with cement and left unpainted;

it looked like the house was under construction. Luckily we had plumbing and did not have to relieve ourselves out in the fields like our neighbours did. That was a privilege because women and young girls can sometimes fall victim to assault and rape when they go out to the fields to relieve themselves.

After school, we would go and play with the cattle and baby goats that the farmers raised. Right behind our house was a large piece of agricultural land or *khet*. Miles and miles of large, barren fields surrounded us and we played on those stretches for hours. The land was hot in the summers, and the winters were equally cold. Most of the youth were now employed in the industrial fields and farming was slowly dying out. Most farmers were under severe debt and their sons now worked in the industrial sector, which had become the main source of employment in Mau Aima. A small unknown village, its main economy depended on the power loom.

The village was so tiny that the judiciary system there was a panchayat. There were no courts. We would sit under a tree, looking up at the village elders, who heard all the cases out one by one. We looked forward to these sessions as a form of entertainment; it befitted our simple village life. My favourite case was of this villager who had kidnapped and brought over his neighbour's cow to be punished. The allegation: the cow would keep eating this man's cattle fodder. The village elders ruled that the owner of the offending cow should keep the animal tied for three days, or until it had learnt its lesson. This cow consequently got special attention from us and we would spoil it rotten in our attempt to deliver it from its misery.

The village also had a tiny forest, which covered around twenty acres of land. As a special treat, my grandparents would take Nargis, Gulshan and me to the forest for picnics on one Sunday every month. Here, we would eat aloo parathas, drink Frooti, and exchange ghost stories. Often we would stumble upon herds of the beautiful, large, timid nilgai.

During my first winter in Mau Aima, I used to struggle to get out of bed. This was my first time experiencing such cold weather. To help us endure the cold better, at night, Dadi – my grandmother – would make us hot Kashmiri kahwa on her chulha.

I turned eleven in October 2007, and in early 2008 things began to change again. It was some time in the beginning of the year that I started to sense a kind of nervous excitement in the family, and this time Gulshan was the reason for the commotion. Her wedding had been arranged with a man called Jamaluddin. He too was from Mau Aima. My father's brother, my Chachu, had arranged the marriage. The family had a good reputation – respectable, kind – and the groom was employed as a salesperson at a store in Mumbai. We had a winner on our hands.

In our community, women are appreciated only twice in their lives: first, when it is time for them to get married, and second, when they give birth to a male heir. When Gulshan's betrothal was announced, people came to our house, laden with jalebis, ladoos, mithai, kheer, and garlands, to congratulate her on a decision well made. The visiting women would say, with a hint of jealousy, that all her dreams were coming true and that they wished the same destiny for their daughters. I'll never forget the number of complaints I heard during those days about unwed twenty-year-old daughters.

Gulshan would emerge dressed in beautiful shalwar-kameezes, her head in a niqab, each time she made an appearance in front of the guests. I was perplexed; I had never seen her cover her head before, even when we had guests.

So many women in India are treated by men as their property. Lucky for me, my brothers and father are the kindest men I have known. However, now that my sister was getting married, the women in our household upheld the accepted traditions of marriage and encouraged the etiquettes of a bride-to-be. Gulshan was both overwhelmed and excited at the prospect of marriage and immersed herself in her soon-to-be-new role – that of a dutiful wife.

On 26 May 2008, hundreds of guests gathered in Mau Aima to attend the nikah of Gulshan and Jamaluddin. The wedding ceremonies lasted for three long but exciting days, and Gulshan's mehendi turned a deep, almost black, shade of red. My mother was relieved to see Gulshan's hands and feet and tipped the mehendi artist generously. Apparently, the darker the mehendi turns, the stronger the marriage will be. Gulshan had turned sixteen that year, and the village women were happy to see that she had ahead of her a promising future with her husband.

At the wedding events of those three days, the men and the women would be seated separately, and it was only during the actual wedding that the bride and the groom came together for the *jab-e-qubul*, or everyone's acceptance of the marriage. Only once they got married were they allowed to move away from their respective segregated areas and sit next to each other. I laughed when I watched them observe each other using mirrors.

My sister was joining a stranger's family and my parents wanted the groom's side to know just how loved she was. For her dowry or *meher*, we gifted Jamaluddin a television, kitchen appliances, jewellery for his sisters and mother, and cash, among other things. I knew this wedding had taken a financial toll on my father, now a mere taxi driver in Mumbai, following the loss of his very own taxi business. However, no expense was spared in ensuring a secure future for Gulshan. My Chachu and my Dadu, Abba's father, sold their own properties to help fund the wedding. The grand wedding was a direct reflection of the status of our family in the village and my grandfather did his due diligence towards his granddaughter. As and when my father received his salary, he paid them back in parts. That's what families did in the village: they helped each other in times of need and a wedding was certainly not the time to scrimp on expenses. Gulshan's lehenga was embroidered with beautiful silk threads; the canopies were a bright red; mist fans were deployed throughout the area to ensure the comfort of the guests. The smell of mutton curry and biryani drifted through the air and every child took second helpings of seekh kebabs and kheer.

Gulshan and Jamaluddin moved to Mumbai later that year to live with Jamaluddin's sister and her husband. Gulshan would gush about her newfound happiness over every telephone conversation with us. Sometime around the middle of August, barely a few months into their marriage, Gulshan announced her pregnancy.

We were ecstatic. The daughter of our family had blessed Jamaluddin's with the announcement of a new member. We carefully arranged baskets of fruit, sweets, and biscuits to take for the expecting family and made a trip to Jamaluddin's sister's house in Mumbai. Such trips were rare for us, because to visit a son-in-law's house without invitation is not exactly appreciated. Gulshan was now part of Jamaluddin's family, and we had to remind ourselves of our limited role in her life. But who can be constantly mindful of tradition when their hands are jittering with excitement?

As we presented the gifts I looked around to catch a glimpse of the house my sister now lived in. It was barren, and the upholstery on the chairs seemed to have been made from ragged pieces of cloth stitched together. We weren't offered tea, food, or even water. I was thirsty, but had been categorically instructed to not ask for anything. Gulshan came forward, her head covered with a dupatta. I rushed towards her the moment she stepped out. 'Gulshan Di, how are you?' I couldn't contain my excitement. I was eleven and I missed my sister terribly. 'Look at my new shalwar suit. Abba bought it especially for me.'

'Reshma, not now,' Gulshan replied, and in that moment I felt as though I was witnessing the rebirth of someone I had known in a previous life. To begin with, she had never covered her head in front of her family, and this new practice seemed odd to me. Ammi quickly pulled me away from my sister and asked me to sit next to her, quietly. 'Children are too outgoing

45

nowadays,' Gulshan's sister-in-law remarked, and I felt an anger bubbling inside me.

It was a formal affair, a short one, and after we left we didn't speak a word about what we saw because we were afraid our emotions would pour out like poison. I overheard Ammi telling Abba that she was worried for Gulshan; if that was how the family treated us, she could not help but wonder about the treatment Gulshan was receiving in that house.

'Maybe they were in a hurry,' Abba said and left it at that. 'Let's not make assumptions based on one meeting alone.'

Constant phone calls, each better than the last, continued to follow. 'I'm fine, I'm happy. Jamaluddin bought me aam papad today; I was really craving some.' Constant reassurances that my pregnant sister was being well looked after were the only reason my mother didn't run over and ask Gulshan to move back in with us, just for a little while, only because she was expecting, and this was, after all, her first pregancy. Usually, a pregnant woman comes back to her *maika* while expecting her first child, but Gulshan refused to do so.

Gulshan's baby was due in April. Nargis, Ammi and I returned to Mumbai for a few days. Ammi wanted to be there when Gulshan gave birth and wished to guide her on motherhood in the days following the birth. Nargis and I excitedly tagged along with Ammi. At last, on 9 April 2009, we received the phone call. I was just twelve, but finally, an aunt! Gulshan had gone into labour and my entire family rushed to Mumbai to be by her side. The image of my father and mother, my brothers, my sister, and me running up and down the hospital corridors searching for cellular network, shouting into our phones to inform relatives of her labour, might have been an amusing sight to a foreigner, but here everyone just ignored us at the maternity ward. Gulshan gave birth to a baby boy. Her first child, and that, too, a boy!

Whatever worries my mother had had for Gulshan, instantly faded away. The mere fact that Saufi was born a healthy boy meant that Gulshan's status in her new family was now absolute. They had no reason to be upset with her, now that her first-born was a son that had arrived in good health. I knew that my mother also heaved a sigh of relief because Gulshan would now have a say in how many more children she and her husband should have. Jamaluddin had five elder sisters before him, the youngest. It was common knowledge that his family had kept having children in the hope that they would one day have a son.

However, the series of events that took place over the next few weeks helped us realize the fallacies of our innocent belief. Gulshan was forced to leave the hospital the same day she gave birth and her husband's family left us stranded with all medical expenses left unpaid.

'She's your daughter,' we were told. 'You have to be responsible for her illnesses.' As if Saufi was an illness! While my parents arranged for funds to pay the bills, we discovered that upon returning to her sister-in-law's home, Gulshan was forced to climb the seven stories to their flat. She was in pain, her legs weak and tired, and she was made to carry Saufi, too. She cried silently as she went up the relentless staircase. A farmer treats his cattle better than her in-laws treated Gulshan.

The next day my mother visited Gulshan at her home. To her horror she found that Gulshan was being denied water and food because she was too tired to cook for the family. That same day my mother travelled back and forth, cooking for Gulshan at our Mumbai home, where my father and my brothers now lived, and carrying those meals and water back to her. The distance each way took over an hour and a half.

My father was deeply disturbed about the state of affairs and insisted that we bring Gulshan and Saufi back to our home. Childbirth is the most painful experience a woman goes through; it's also an event that warrants unprecedented love, attention, and care for the mother, but Gulshan was somehow in anguish. After five days of to and fro to help Gulshan through this time and witnessing the painful treatment she received, Ammi decided it was time to bring her daughter and infant grandson to our home and have them stay there until Gulshan regained her strength. But how would one accomplish this without offending Gulshan's in-laws? A plan was hatched. As per the Muslim customs we followed, the birth of a child ought to be celebrated. To that end, my father borrowed money from Dadu. He called Jamaluddin over and offered to pay for the *akikah* – the ceremony to celebrate the birth of a child by sacrificing an animal, as well as the naming ceremony – and lessen the burden on his son-in-law. Hearing this, Jamaluddin agreed to send Gulshan and Saufi to her parents' home and said that he would visit with his family on the day of the akikah. And this is how Ammi was able to bring Gulshan and Saufi home so they could finally be well looked after.

The seventh day since childbirth is considered the most auspicious day for the akikah. A lamb was slaughtered in accordance with the Prophet's Sunnah (verbally transmitted records of his teachings) and the meat was shared generously before the child was given a name that still rings in our ears with longing. This day was supposed to be perfect. The safeguarding of a new son for Gulshan. Little did she know that years later this ceremony would be seen as worthless, and she would long to hear the sound of her son's voice.

After the ceremony, Jamaluddin asked my mother to send Gulshan and his son back to his house. I remember this day clearly because my father said no. His daughter had been raised with so much love and care that he could not torment her by sending her back into this marriage. Even though he had offered to pay for the ceremony he was shocked that Jamaluddin had accepted the offer so quickly. He began to sense that Gulshan had no economic independence whatsoever in that household. However, nothing could be done. She was a married woman and our neighbours and friends advised Gulshan to return. Things are supposed to get better after one has a child. Her husband had asked for Gulshan to be returned. My mother, too, insisted that Gulshan should go back and Gulshan acquiesced. What I remember most vividly is how I never heard her opinion in this matter. She said she was 'happy' to go back and then, suddenly, she was gone.

One year later, in June 2010, Jamaluddin lost his job. It was then that we started noticing glaring discrepancies in what Gulshan would tell us about her life and the actual reality. One day, Gulshan came to our house and sat my father down. She was crying as she said, 'Abba, you help everyone. Why don't you help me?' She needed money.

My father was shattered. He felt he had not paid enough attention to Gulshan's situation, possibly because she was now married. He grappled with his guilt. 'Of course, beta,' he said as he hugged her tight. 'How much do you want?' He handed Nargis a cheque. 'Here, take Nargis to the bank. She'll withdraw money for you.'

But Nargis returned without Gulshan. The minute she had handed Gulshan the cash, Jamaluddin had appeared out of nowhere and snatched it. My parents didn't sleep the entire night, worried that Jamaluddin was harassing Gulshan for money. He was in fact doing exactly that.

A few weeks later, the demand for money increased. 'Her dowry wasn't enough. She spends too much. We're feeding her, aren't we; do you think that comes cheap?' My father tried to meet their growing demands, denying himself basic needs, because he could not witness his daughter being treated in this unworthy manner. He bought cheaper medicines, stopped drinking tea even when he went on sixteen-hour shifts, and did not buy a new shirt for years.

Sometime in July that year, Jamaluddin decided to move back to Mau Aima to live with his parents because he could no longer afford to live in Mumbai without a salary. Although he lived with his sister and her husband in Mumbai, the fact that he was the unemployed brother of the woman of the house diminished his power in the scheme of things. Gulshan's sister-in-law could no longer house them there, and Jamaluddin did not have enough money to pay rent. There was never an option for them to stay with us. A married woman and her husband never stay with her parents, not unless they are unafraid of answering questions regarding the husband's incapability to earn and provide for the family.

My father refused to let Gulshan go. He feared for her. Something gnawed at him; a gut feeling, in retrospect. He could still identify at Jamaluddin's end a semblance of respect for the male members of our family, but would the degree of separation reduce his fear to ashes and only result in Gulshan being further mistreated?

Despite these misgivings, Ammi, Nargis, and I continued to live in Mau Aima. We visited Mumbai on short holidays, and always had a home there. Ammi told Abba not to worry since we would be there to look out for Gulshan. But the same old story unfolded yet again. Gulshan was married with a son. A child needed a father, and what would people say? Also, Gulshan had never expressed her wish to end the marriage. She took Saufi and went to Mau Aima with Jamaluddin to live with his parents.

My brothers and father continued to work in Mumbai. But we would meet Gulshan. Sometimes she would mention difficulties with her in-laws, but in India, especially rural and small-town India, that is often an acceptable conflict considering so many couples live with the husband's family and the wife has to adjust to her in-laws' way of life and new family traditions.

In August 2010, we received news of Gulshan's second pregnancy. Her family attempted to illegally determine the sex of the baby, but failed.

On 10 April 2011, we received news that Gulshan had given birth to a beautiful baby girl, whom they named Riza. Abba, Riyaz, and Aizaz were in Mumbai and they could not wait to come visit their granddaughter. They started coming to see us often in Mau Aima and, on such visits, Gulshan would bring Saufi and Riza to our home. We never went to her in-laws' residence because we feared it would lead to Gulshan being mistreated again. The true extent of the vicious violence that was being carried out against her was still unknown to my family. In order to protect us, Gulshan never shared her troubles with us to a great extent. We would keep asking after her and only receive tight-lipped responses – none that could help us truly determine the state of affairs.

Then, two years later, on a hot summer morning in May 2013, we received a devastating phone call from Gulshan's neighbours. I remember how young I was, sixteen to be exact. I was confused as my mother started shouting into the phone. Her words woke me and Nargis up, and we jumped out of bed and went to sit by our mother's side.

'They'll kill her, they'll kill her!' she screamed. 'Go, get Gulshan and the children right now! They're going to kill her!' My father quickly grabbed his wallet and ran, without asking a single question. We were lucky Abba was visiting us during my summer holidays.

We never even had to ask who 'they' were. We rushed outside, waiting for Abba to come back, hopefully with Gulshan and her kids. Soon, an auto pulled up from the direction of Gulshan's in-laws' residence. We saw a woman jump out and run towards us. It was Gulshan. My father followed right behind. Her clothes, soaking wet, hung from her ragged body, Saufi was crying as he couldn't keep pace with his mother, while Riza howled in her arms. Abba picked up Saufi and ushered them into our house. As she came closer, I felt faint.

She reeked of kerosene. Then it hit me: she was drenched from head to toe in kerosene. They had tried to burn her alive. We rushed her and the children inside and locked all doors and windows. My mother kept crying, as she tried to scrub Gulshan clean with a towel, but the smell just couldn't be suppressed.

That night, my father received a phone call from Jamaluddin's neighbours who related the events to him. Jamaluddin's parents had doused Gulshan in kerosene because she refused to ask my father for more money. They were about to set her on fire when she grabbed hold of Saufi and Riza. With their grandson in her arms, they paused, taken aback, and Gulshan seized this opportunity to run and hide in the neighbours' home. The neighbours had called and alerted Ammi of the situation. While Gulshan's in-laws were looking for her and the children, she had snuck out from the neighbours' backdoor in the morning, knowing that we had been informed, and ran towards our home. By then Abba had already rushed to her aid.

Gulshan just sat in shocked silence, tears pouring down her eyes. Nargis and I didn't leave her alone for a second because we were scared that she might hurt herself. My mother was with the children, trying to calm them down. Riza was two and even her heart was throbbing out of shock. She couldn't breathe and my mother kept trying to get her to drink water lest she become dehydrated.

It is Riza's image that haunts me the most even today. She had large blisters all over her arms, her back, and around her neck. Big, ugly boils.

4

Talaq, Talaq, Talaq

OVER THE NEXT FEW days my family tried to make sense of Gulshan's awful predicament by gathering together as much information as possible with the fewest questions they could ask. My mother was weighed down by guilt and my father was still in shock. Had they missed the signs?

The most worrisome situation at hand was not how Gulshan's marriage had unravelled into this disastrous state. Rather, it was our constant worry over Riza's condition. She was just a child and to watch her suffer like this was heart-wrenching for all of us. Her little body was covered with sweltering red blisters and for days she ran a temperature between 102 and 104 degrees. Gulshan would bathe her in cold water, attempting to lower her temperature, because no medication was working. Her boils were dabbed with Lacto Calamine. Riza never cried. To me it seemed as if she didn't want to irritate us. The poor child had been at the receiving end of unwarranted anger numerous times before.

After the trauma, Gulshan's painful memories had been clouded by an ardent wish to forget. But she was able to tell us a few things. Riza's birth had not been celebrated because of her gender, and with her birth Gulshan's power in the household had diminished as she was now the mother of a daughter. For the last one year, Saufi had had a room to sleep in, while Gulshan and Riza were forced to sleep on hard mats in the common room. To protect Riza, Gulshan had strategized a policy of minimum requests, just enough to ensure a reasonable life for her daughter while keeping in mind the tipping point leading to a violent outcome.

But then Riza's health started to decline and would constantly be ill. Gulshan begged for Riza to be shown to a doctor, but her mother-in-law scorned at the thought. 'Why waste money on showing her to doctor? She's fine, children get sick.'

So, Gulshan tried to hide away some money. Her plan was to save enough coins, spare change, and lie about the household budget, just until she could save enough to take Riza to the hospital. That never happened. Her plan was discovered and her in-laws confiscated the funds and stripped Gulshan of managing any household expenses at all. Her mother-in-law took over the kitchen budget, and Gulshan and Riza were now allowed only leftovers from the family meals.

Gulshan begged and cried to have Riza taken to the hospital, and when her requests were denied yet again she broke down in defeat. She monitored her daughter's temperature hourly, tried to medicate her at home, away from the prying eyes of her family, and planned to go to the neighbours for help. She never informed us because she feared if Jamaluddin found out she had reached out to us behind his back, he would divorce her and never allow her to see Saufi again.

But all I kept wondering was how we had missed all the signs. I can never allay the feelings of guilt that had overwhelmed my family. Their very loved daughter and grandchildren were being abused without our knowledge – Ammi blamed herself and wondered if the family's behaviour during Saufi's birth justified asking for a separation, while Abba blamed himself for allowing Gulshan to move to Mau Aima.

Since Gulshan had moved in with us, my mother had forbidden us from asking too many questions; it made my sister nervous. My mother wanted Gulshan to feel safe. Human nature is such that it shies away from change, and Gulshan had lost far too much in much too short a time. She needed some semblance of normality, a sharp contradiction to her recent trauma.

So, for the first few days we didn't ask any probing questions. The only thing, or person, that we inquired after was Riza. She was unwell and we had taken her to a doctor. All we had to do now was wait for the medicines to work.

Around three or four days after they moved here, my mother poured Gulshan a steaming cup of tea after the children had been put to bed. At first, there was tension in the air. Gulshan didn't touch her tea. 'Your tea will get cold,' I said. 'I'm waiting for exactly that to happen,' she said.

'Here, let me cool it for you,' said my mother as she reached for the cup. When we were young she would pour the tea from cup to saucer and saucer to cup until it cooled down. 'No, don't worry about it,' said Gulshan, and took a sip of the hot tea. This was how it was with Gulshan, her settling for everything because she thought that accommodating her wishes may be too much of a burden on us. Over the past few days, whenever we asked her what she would like to eat or what time she would like to be woken up the next day, her response would be for us to do as we pleased. Watching her like this made me sad, as though she had forgotten that she had a choice in life. I tried telling her that 'whatever' wasn't on the menu, but my half-hearted joke fell on deaf ears.

Many questions were left unanswered, but sometimes silence can hint at unspoken pain. We drank our tea under the pretence of relaxation and talked about our day, laughed at the funny faces Saufi made, and thanked Allah for allowing Riza a peaceful night after many nights of distress. However, what needed to be asked most was sitting impatiently on our tongues, trying to ignore the unease in our hearts. We didn't know if we wanted the answers, but were certain that we must have them.

At last, my mother placed her hand over Gulshan's. Gulshan tried to pull away, but my mother only held it tighter – a gesture of protection. No matter what happened, we weren't leaving her side.

Gulshan took a deep breath and released it in broken whimpers. Tears began to flow down her cheeks. Muffled sounds escaped her mouth; she had forgotten what it was like to be heard. Crying aloud must have felt like an assault to her newfound invisibility. My mother gently patted her back and assured her, 'We're here, right here. Just tell us what you need. I love you. I am so sorry. I love you. Abba and I want you to be free, Gulshan. And we want you to know that you and the children will always have a home here with us.'

My mother is the kind of person who hushes away tears with a simple 'don't cry'. This time, however, she did not. I was surprised at how long Ammi held Gulshan's hand and let her cry, not once asking her to stop. Some things warrant tears and my mother knew that Gulshan would drown if she didn't let hers flow. She had reached the human limit to bear pain and my mother wanted to give her the release she so desperately needed. For once, it was Gulshan who spoke first.

'They've tried to kill me before.'

My mother sat up straighter, her hand still clutching Gulshan's. I felt a painful lump at the back of my throat and had so much to say, but feared that I would break down. We remained quiet. 'He used to hit me earlier, over money. I asked for as much as I could, but it wasn't fair to Abba and you. When we moved to Mau Aima, his mother and father backed his demands. Soon they demanded a car. "Jamaluddin doesn't have a job and why should he have the luxuries he hasn't worked for?" I would ask myself. I told them this once and that was when they slammed my head against the wall. For the next week they made me cut wood for hours without any help. My arms hurt and my feet were swollen. When I came back inside I was forced to cook, and if I sat down for even five minutes they would deny me the chance to spend time with my children. His mother would take them away and make them sleep in her room, leaving me helpless without them in my sight. I was so scared, Ammi, I was so scared.'

That night, Gulshan spoke of all the abuse she had suffered at the hands of this cruel and violent family. One of Jamaluddin's sisters was having an affair with a local politician. His wife had burnt herself to death after speaking up against the affair. A case of murder was filed against the politician, but he was never taken to court because the death was eventually deemed a suicide. His family was dangerous and the people in his inner circle could be best described as glorified goons.

Gulshan was emotionally abused and constantly told that she should try to maintain her spirits, lest her parents receive an untimely call about her 'suicide'.

She was trapped. She prayed that things would get better. There were times when Jamaluddin was kind. He occasionally allowed her to eat a meal of her choice and sometimes even asked her to sleep in his bed. Gulshan truly believed that their love was strong and that he was simply under the influence of his family for him to be able to treat her the way he did. Eventually though, she could see no way out, and was forced to run for her life when she knew she was on the brink of death.

We listened to her story that night in shocked silence. I fell asleep with just one thought on my mind. *What if she hadn't escaped, what if we hadn't been in Mau Aima that night? Would we have received a call about her 'suicide'?*

The next morning, I believe my mother repeated Gulshan's story to my father. For it was decided that the children and Gulshan would continue to live in Mau Aima at our family home. They were to never return to Jamaluddin again.

This was the beginning of a new life for Gulshan and her kids. Initially, the children wondered why they weren't going home to their father, but soon the comfort of a peaceful environment made the questions fade out. They were happy and wanted to hold on to the calm for as long as they could. We decided they must have as normal a life as possible, and that meant they would be going to school.

It was over the next few weeks that I began to notice gradual changes in Gulshan. She was now laughing a fuller laugh and, at times, there was that air of charming innocence that had always surrounded her. A few days later, she made chicken biryani and gave the leftovers to a beggar on the street. That was a happy day for her. She probably never had the power to make such decisions in her marital home.

Sixteen was a particularly challenging age for me. I would say that I was made aware of my limitations at sixteen. For the first time in my life, I was witnessing unimaginable cruelty against a woman I loved and admired. I realized that none of us was invincible. No woman was safe. Since Gulshan's return, I would be filled with rage often. Cold, hard rage that would make my hands shake and kindle red sparks in my vision as my head felt as though it would burst from the throbbing pain in my temples. Anger and helplessness can do that sometimes.

Women we knew visited when they had some free time; some came out of concern, some out of boredom, some simply for gossip. However, I always knew the ones who came for help. They never asked for help, but I could tell that's why they came. They listened to Gulshan, silent tears streaming down their cheeks. These were tears of empathy; they knew just what Gulshan had gone through.

There was once a woman who came to talk about a 'friend' whose husband beat her – she refused to cut her hair short after her in-laws complained she was using too much shampoo. After she would wash the dishes, her in-laws would check how much soap she had used. She had no parents or siblings. This young woman's immediate family had abandoned her after paying her meagre dowry. She had nowhere to go. She couldn't escape the oppression of her abusive in-laws because her aunts and uncles believed that they had done their duty by paying her dowry and that she now belonged with her husband and her new family. But the bruises she tried to cover on her arms didn't escape my notice.

These women who came for help kept me awake at night. It made me sad to realize that so many women had no power over their own lives and that the only succour they had was derived from listening to stories from other women in similar states of misery. It was as if they were finding comfort in their despair, and the more stories they shared, the more courage they found in each other as sisters.

Over time, Gulshan and her children settled into a routine. The children would go to school, while Gulshan would start going about her chores in the house. Jamaluddin was a ghost sailing into the past. That was until 28 April 2014.

This was the day Jamaluddin called out of the blue, and in a house filled with people, it was Gulshan who happened to pick up the phone. 'Talaq, talaq, talaq,' he screamed. Until 22 August 2017, triple talaq was recognized as a legitimate method of effecting divorce among Muslims. All a Muslim man had to do was utter the word 'talaq' thrice and he would be legally free from his marriage.

On hearing those words, Gulshan began quivering with rage. Even towards the end of their relationship, Jamaluddin had once again proven his power over her. He had stripped her of her right to divorcing him; in any case, it would have been a lengthier and a far more undignified process had she, the wife, initiated the process. But at least Gulshan would have had peace in knowing that she was the one seeking separation because of all the abuse she had suffered. What right did Jamaluddin even have to seek talaq from Gulshan? By initiating divorce, Jamaluddin had made it clear that he had issues with their marriage, and grievances against his wife. Once again, he had tarnished Gulshan's reputation.

Gulshan was devastated. While she had found freedom for her oppressive marriage at last, I believe, secretly she truly wished for Jamaluddin to turn into the man she had once loved. She believed that the time they had spent apart would perhaps change him for the better and that things would go back to normal – whatever 'normal' meant.

Those days were difficult. Emotions ran high and moods often swung out of our control. At last, after days of discussing the pros and cons, we realized that the divorce had come as a blessing in disguise. My parents continued to remind Gulshan of her worth. Jamaluddin, who found it so easy to discard the mother of his children over the phone, without any attempt at mending their marriage, was surely not worthy of Gulshan.

A week later he called again, demanding to see the children. Gulshan refused. She was afraid if she allowed her children to visit their father, she would never see them again. She had been denied time with Saufi and Riza while she lived with her husband. Only a naive divorced woman would believe that her children, once in their father's home, would be sent back to live with their mother.

The calls soon became more frequent, threatening, urgent, and desperate. One minute Jamaluddin would be threatening us with legal action, the next he would appeal to our morality. At times he begged Gulshan to return to him, apologizing profusely for the way he had handled things. He begged to overturn the divorce he had so effortlessly and viciously spat on Gulshan. As easy as it had been for him to divorce Gulshan, it was just as hard for her to accept his apologies.

His pleas and threats fell on deaf ears, mostly because of my parents who had now become Gulshan's iron cast, holding her up even when she thought she would break. Apart from the frequent phone calls, our life carried on more or less smoothly.

After we would wake up in the morning, Gulshan and Ammi would prepare hot tea for everyone which we would drink with buttered rusks. The children would beg for five extra minutes in bed and Gulshan would have to rush them out the door for school. I would leave for school a little earlier. Gulshan would pick them up from school since their classes ended before mine. One day when Gulshan went to pick the kids up, Riza rushed into her arms, complaining about how hungry she was. Gulshan laughed and promised her biryani for lunch. All they had to do was wait for Saufi and then head home. He was usually late, his friends often holding him up for one reason or another. But that day, after she had already waited ten minutes, Gulshan began to feel worried. Why was there still no sign of Saufi? Gulshan picked Riza up in her arms made her way to Saufi's classroom, only to find it empty. She hurried down the corridors towards the teachers' meeting room, where she found one of his teachers and asked her about Saufi.

'Saufi? Oh, his father picked him up earlier today. He was crying and refused to go with him, but I assumed that was because he was unwell. His father told me he was unwell.'

My sister felt paralyzed with panic. Holding Riza in her arms, she ran outside, flagged down an auto, and came back home in tears. 9 May 2014. It's a date we still remember with horror, the date on which Saufi got kidnapped.

We were all preparing lunch when Gulshan returned. Her hair was a wild mess and she was talking breathlessly. None of us could understand what she was saying. She was running around the house, looking for her bag, some money, the phone. 'What happened, Gulshan?' my mother asked over and over again. 'Where is Saufi? Gulshan, is he alright?'

'Jamaluddin picked him up from school today. He took him. He took Saufi,' said Gulshan at last.

'What?' my mother screeched as she reached for the phone. She called out to my father who was outside, attending to some chores. We were lucky that he happened to be visiting us from Mumbai at the time.

Abba instructed all of us to stay inside the house. Ammi and he would go to Gulshan's in-laws'. He forbade Gulshan from following them. We waited impatiently for over two hours. Gulshan wouldn't speak; she was crying silent tears. I don't think she was even aware that she was crying.

When Abba and Ammi returned we knew we had lost Saufi. He wasn't with them. What was even more haunting were the details that emerged. When my parents reached Jamaluddin's house, Saufi was already there. They weren't allowed in and Jamaluddin, his father, mother, and sisters, congregated outside, in the garden. They physically barred my parents from entering the house, verbally abused them, and even hit my mother when she begged for Saufi to be returned so he could be with Gulshan. Saufi, upon hearing the commotion, rushed outdoors, wailing for his mother. As he was reaching for Ammi's arms, Jamaluddin's mother picked up the distraught child, took him inside and locked the doors. Jamaluddin physically threw my parents out of the house. There was nothing more to be done.

My parents were outnumbered and, knowing how violent Jamaluddin's family could be, my father did not wish to put my mother at further harm. They returned without Saufi, but his wails haunted them for nights to come. The only course of action now was to place their trust in the police. The same evening, Gulshan filed a case against Jamaluddin on grounds of kidnapping.

The next few days passed in a series of confused conversations. My father would keep going to the police station for updates (of which there were none), my sister would call every member of Jamaluddin's family one after another (all her calls went unanswered), and the neighbours would be unhelpful, offering only fake 'tips' about Saufi's whereabouts that they had supposedly heard through the grapevine. By the end of each day all of us would sit shattered, having gone over the minutest details of every conversation any of us had with anyone who could help. Advice was in abundance, but always unhelpful. At least the fatigue helped Gulshan sleep. It kept her sane.

At last, after days of looking for a way forward, we received a phone call from the police station on 18 May 2014. They asked us to reach the Allahabad High Court the very next day. The police gave us no further details. They just said that Saufi would now be in their care and we could finally bring him home. We didn't ask any further questions because we were grateful enough to know that the police were doing their job and didn't wish to waste their time. I had my Alimah exam the next day but, in the midst of all the excitement at home, I put my books away without a second thought. Saufi, my nephew, was finally returning home.

5

When It Rains, It Pours

I TURNED TO MY right and pulled the thin cotton sheet over my head, nestling my face into the crook of my left arm, searching for complete darkness. I wasn't ready to get out of bed yet.

'Reshma, my girl, it's time to get up,' said my mother, gently tapping me on the shoulder. 'Five more minutes,' I insisted. I heard her mumble something about my indolence as she got up so she could move on to whatever it was she had to do next at 6 a.m. on a Monday morning.

I have never been much of a morning person. My ideal day would have me sleeping in until noon or later. Unfortunately, on that day, I had no choice. The date, 19 May 2014, would prove to be significant for three reasons, and on that particular morning, I was still unaware of the third and most harrowing one.

I suddenly felt the need to look for my phone, to step out of bed, take a bath. A surge of panic and excitement took over me, driving away all drowsiness. Phone in hand, I mindlessly went through the text messages from the previous week, trying in vain to distract myself from my anxiety. My Alimah exam was today, and a crippling fear had me in its grips since the previous night. There was a strange foreboding in my chest and I was certain it was a warning that I would fail my exam. My panic clashed with another kind of excitement, a much happier one – my sister was going to pick Saufi up from the police station and bring him home today.

My five extra minutes were up sooner than I had expected and I forced myself out of bed. I winced at the slight creak the floor made upon contact with my feet. My Chacha's son was still sleeping next to me. For a moment I felt jealous of my cousin. The memories of my carefree childhood days swept over me. There had been no exams, no expectations, no sacrifices made by my family to ensure my bright and successful future.

I ignored the voice in my head that tried to convince me to get back into bed for a final five more minutes. Not today, I told myself. I had worked far too hard for my Alimah exam and the promise of seeing my nephew in the evening meant that the day had to pass by as quickly as possible.

Looking back, I often wonder if this had been Mistake Number One.

I stumbled through the darkness and made my way to the bathroom. Gulshan was washing dishes in the kitchen. She must have noticed me skulking because she looked up from the sink and smiled. 'How are you feeling?' she said, her cheeriness foiling my attempt at avoiding conversation.

'Nervous,' I said, as I quickly walked off before she could respond or ask more questions. The morning call for prayer that day had sent a chill down my spine. The mu'adhin's first call to prayer was normally a blanket of solace to my mind. But today, I missed Mumbai.

I wasn't nervous. I was terrified. I rushed into the bathroom and brushed my teeth. I stared at myself in the mirror, my left hand gripping the sink with a numbing force.

I wasn't nervous. I was sad. My breathing was shallow and my heart was sinking. I reminded myself to breathe. I played a game. I looked in the mirror and stopped breathing, trying to see how long I could go without taking a breath. I stopped playing when the pale blue light from the only bulb above the sink began to merge with the fire-blazing reds that were now playing tricks with my oxygen-deprived brain. I don't remember how long it took before I gave in and decided that this game wasn't worth fainting for.

I decided not to have a bath. It would be sensible to focus on my exam now, and have my bath before afternoon prayers at the mosque. I suddenly longed for my father, who was now back working in Mumbai. If he had been with me he would have made a bad joke or two and helped me feel better.

It's just an exam, I said to myself, as I finally left the bathroom after changing into Gulshan's niqab. I had forgotten to ask Abba to bring my old niqab from Mumbai and had bought a new one, but I wasn't going to wear it unless there was a special reason, so Gulshan had offered me one of hers.

I later wondered if accepting my sister's niqab had been Mistake Number Two.

I stepped out into the living room where Gulshan was putting on her own niqab. 'Hurry, Reshma, we'll get late,' she said, without a hint of anger in her voice.

I knew that her interest in being on time had little to do with my exam. But of course I did not mind. I was happy for my sister. I had witnessed her mapping out uncharacteristic revenge plots the past few days and seen a sad, ugly side to her that no one should have to witness in a person they love. But today Gulshan was herself again. She was finally going to see her son. She had to be at the court by 11 a.m.

Still, my palms continued to sweat, and her happiness was not as infectious for me as it should have been.

'Beta, drink some tea and eat this,' said my mother, offering me a steaming cup of sweet tea and some toast. I quickly sipped the tea, my tongue singing from the heat. I took a bite of the toast without saying a word. Before I could object, my mother rushed towards me again, this time with a bowl of dahi and sugar and shoved a spoonful into my mouth, apparently to ward off evil.

'Is everything alright?' my mother asked, placing her hand on my forehead to check my temperature. She would often do this, always associating uncharacteristic behaviour with illness. 'Are you still nervous?'

'I don't know what it is, Ammi. I'm afraid I may fail, or that something worse might happen.' My voice was shaking, and I felt a lump in my throat. 'Shh …' Ammi shushed me, as she held my face in her hands. 'If you're not sure, don't go, beta. It's just an exam. You can take it another time. Stay here. We'll wait for Saufi together.'

I knew my mother probably thought that all the emotions from the past two days were overwhelming me. So much had happened – from Saufi's kidnapping to discovering that he had been rescued to making plans for his big return.

'Or I can come with you,' Ammi offered. I nodded.

Without wasting a moment, my mother put on her hijab. Just then, my neighbours and friends, Firdoz and Afroz, came knocking at the door. Gulshan let them in and I told them that I had no wish to take the exam.

'But we've worked so hard, Reshma,' said Firdoz. 'We'll all be writing the same paper,' said Afroz. It won't be so bad, was the general consensus and it was too late to back out now anyway. Everyone, including my mother, was ready to leave the house.

That's when Riza began to cry. 'If I go, there will be no one to take care of Riza,' said my mother, as she picked up her granddaughter and tried to pacify her in the midst of all the commotion. But Riza was inconsolable, so my mother decided to stay back knowing Riza would find comfort only with Gulshan or herself.

'I might as well get it over with along with everyone else. Take care of Riza,' I said to my mother as I followed Gulshan, Firdoz, and Afroz out of the house. Our exam was at 8 a.m. and we had quite a distance to cover.

We set off in two pairs. Gulshan walked ahead with Firdoz, while Afroz and I walked behind at a much slower pace. The streets were so narrow that walking side by side with Afroz was challenging. I kept glancing back to make sure there was no ambitious vehicle attempting to make its way down the constricting road.

I remember being surprised by the incredible resolve of a strange old man wheeling a large vegetable cart. His eyes were withdrawn, defeated almost, and his knees seemed as if they would buckle any moment under the pressure of all the weight he was pulling. In the midst of all the clamour around him – bikes trying to swerve past him, stray dogs barking wildly to protect their territories, women shouting at their children to quickly finish tending to the animals before heading off to school, and men hurriedly trying to set up their shops or flag down rickshaws so they could go to work – this man seemed to be walking at his own slow, sort of defeated pace.

Mau Aima was not Mumbai, but in essence it wasn't all that different from the neighbourhood we used to live in. I guess no matter where we end up in life, time waits for no one, so we make our peace with it and understand that time itself will dictate what we do with it as it quietly brings us closer to death. This man didn't deserve this sorry place in the world. Looking at his forlorn body I could tell that he had paid his dues. I wondered where his family was.

Suddenly my hands felt kind of empty and I forgot what I had been thinking about. I reached into my handbag. 'Allah, I've forgotten my phone at home,' I shouted as I grabbed Afroz's arm. 'I *have* to go back and get it.'

I never left home without my phone.

Afroz waited as I searched through my bag again. Gulshan and Firdoz walked back to where we were to find out what was holding us up. 'I'll just rush home and get my phone. I'll make it quick, promise. You three carry on or you'll be late for the exam,' I said as I closed my bag.

'That makes no sense,' said Gulshan. 'All of us are here, why do you need your phone? You can use ours.'

I knew there was no point arguing because it was clear Afroz, Firdoz, and Gulshan were getting annoyed with the delay I was causing. I told myself I wouldn't really need my phone during the exam anyway.

I realized later this was Mistake Number Three.

We went on our way, and soon arrived at the local market. It was located right next to the Mau Aima train station, so even though it was only 7:30 in the morning, the place was already bustling. Women in worn-down saris were hawking oranges, bananas, apples, and imitation jewellery. '*Beta, bohni ka waqt hai*,' said an old lady who was selling embroidered shoes. I shouldn't have stopped to admire them because I felt guilty for not being able to purchase a single pair and help her out a little. It is a common belief amongst the Mau Aima street vendors, just like it is with vendors all over India, that the bohni, or the first sale, is the luckiest sale of the day.

The street was narrow, and bikers constantly whizzed by too dangerously close for my comfort. But the loud, blaring honks of the motorbikes, autos, and rickshaws did not faze me.

The right side of the street was filled with vendors. We walked on the left, where the remains of an old, dilapidated red brick wall still stood, perhaps built by the Mughals, or maybe even the British. I had no idea, but I knew it could not have been built after India's independence. It just stood there, neglected, but lent us support as we plastered ourselves against it occasionally to allow the larger four-wheelers to pass.

As we continued walking, I suddenly thought I saw a familiar face pass by on a bike. It looked like my brother-in-law Jamaluddin's nephew. That can't be right, I thought to myself, as I kept pace with Afroz, while Gulshan and Firdoz walked ahead.

The sequence of events that took place next has seared itself into my memory; it is like a haunting film set that keeps playing on loop. Someone once asked me why I like to watch the same movies over and over again, and I had said it's because I like the comfort of knowing what happens next. In this case, I later found myself revisiting the events over and over again to try and work out how things could have gone very differently.

I watched Gulshan stop in her tracks, next to the five-foot wall. She looked at it as someone called out to her, and from where I stood, it seemed as if a few bricks had fallen off from the centre of the wall, creating a hole through which one could see on the other side.

I watched Gulshan reach out for something through that gap in the wall, and the world went dark for a microsecond. I realized I had simply blinked, and during that briefest of moments, my life derailed into complete darkness.

As it turns out, Jamaluddin had been hiding behind the brick wall and had carefully removed all the weak bricks from the centre, so he could keep an eye on the passers-by. In his hand was a bottle brimming with what looked like a vicious liquid. When Gulshan noticed a hand reach out through the wall and realized it was Jamaluddin's, she sensed danger right away. He was going to direct the contents of the bottle at her, but she reached out and grabbed his hand just in time, and managed to divert his aim.

The liquid was intended for her face, but as she kept her determined grip on the bottle, the acid began to pour down her arm.

I watched her buckle. Her elbow bent in pain, she clutched her burning arm and screamed with a desperation I had never witnessed before in my life. 'Run, Reshma, run,' she shouted. 'Run, Reshma, run, run, run,' she went on.

I froze momentarily, and then realized the urgency of the situation. I knew I had to run as though my life depended upon it. I could feel the blood rushing to my ears and the world around me ceased to exist. My survival instinct kicked in, just as I remembered Jamaluddin's nephew's face.

Firdoz was with Gulshan, and I had to save myself. I whirled turned around to find myself facing two men on a motorbike. I recognized them both: one was Jamaluddin's cousin and the other his nephew, both of whom had dismounted and were now running towards me. I suddenly felt trapped and turned around to find Jamaluddin also running towards me from the other end. Gulshan made to run after him, but she was delirious with pain, still clutching her arm as though it was her own crumbling spirit.

The panic, the uncertainty, the shock of it all, made me lose precious moments. The nephew and the cousin had already grabbed me from behind; they were tugging at my hair from over my sister's niqab and pushing me down to the ground. The men were heavy and strong, but still I tried to fight them off, clawed them with my bare hands, but my physical strength was at best a feeble shadow compared to those monsters. I was, after all, just seventeen.

For a brief second, I managed to open my mouth and take in a few gasps of air. I tried to scream, but was unable to produce any sound. I believe that was my body's way of telling me that I needed to save all my strength for the screams that would later traumatize me for nights without end.

The men were now on top of me. Jamaluddin's cousin grabbed my hands and pulled them over my head, so there was no way I could fight. Without even removing my niqab, he emptied over my face the contents of a flask he had been carrying.

I remember wondering why they would throw warm water on my face, but that thought lasted only for a heavenly fraction of a second. I wish that the embarrassment of being treated like an animal, being pushed to the ground, and having an offensive liquid poured over my face, was all I would have to deal with.

But within moments I could hear at a distance a strange, terrified, unnatural, desperate scream. It was me. I was on fire, and the haunting screams were erupting from my own being. Even if I practised hard I could never again scream the way I did that day. Even the devil would cover his ears if he had heard me that day.

I have later wondered if I should have slept in for those five extra minutes, worn my new burqa, stayed back with my mother, turned around for my cell phone, stopped and bought those shoes, or haggled over an apple.

Perhaps if I had done all those things, I would never have been attacked with acid.

They never even removed the niqab first so they could look at my face.

6

Afterlife

I DON'T KNOW IF you've ever smoked a cigarette, but I sure haven't. I have however witnessed floating stray cigarette embers falling on smokers' hands and thighs and they just sit there, blowing at the burns, wincing laughingly at the pain. I used to wince with them out of sympathy and camaraderie, but now such burns are inconsequential to me.

The sound of my screams still sends shivers down my own spine. Similar to the flash of lightning we see before a storm, I witnessed my own doom before my screams shattered my surroundings. My attack happened faster than lightning itself, but the thunder has gone on and a heavy cloud of pain still hangs over me.

The two men pulled my hair back, pushed me to the ground, poured acid all over my face, and disappeared as quickly as they had arrived on the scene. A few flicks of their wrists is all it took to induce a storm in my life. A watch glistened at the corner of my eye as the hand drew away from my face, quick as lightning.

Lightning strikes first, and then comes thunder. You see the precursor of damage before you truly grasp, hear, feel, or understand the aftermath to come. My screams erupted just as the watch disappeared, irrefutable proof of the violence that had been unleashed on my life.

The first thing I noticed was my niqab melting off my face. Then came the smell of burning flesh. Mine. All this while I couldn't stop screaming. I screamed in shock as they threw me to the ground. I screamed in pain as they poured acid on me. Slithering on the ground I clawed at the melting niqab like a rabid animal. I screamed in anger and I writhed in agony over the loss of my dignity. For the first time in my life I had absolutely no control over my body.

Acid is a corrosive substance, one that can even burn through metal. And I am only made of flesh and bones. If a person who has been attacked with acid can get access to water within three seconds, the damage can be controlled. But no one threw water on me, not then, not until hours later.

The initial sensation was that of drowning in ice. The acid burnt so hotly and sent my mind into such a delirium that I mistook it for iciness. That comparably pleasant sensation lasted for milliseconds and soon I began to feel as if I was burning in hellfire. I know now that the initial confusion was due to my pumping adrenaline, my body's attempt to gauge the true extent of the damage.

The acid began to eat away at my face. Pain shot through my body as though I was being shredded alive. I guess in a way that was true. The acid was eating through the layers of my skin and before long it aimed for my bones. My flesh was giving way. My vision went foggy from the relentless pain. It was so intense, so severe, that those few minutes felt like a lifetime, and I wished for death.

If not for the adrenalin, I would probably have died from shock. Gulshan, Firdoz and Afroz had witnessed everything and now ran towards me. They kept screaming my name, rubbing my face in their attempt to wipe off the liquid. But it only went deeper and also managed to burn Gulshan's hand.

The memory is like an elusive dream, but I faintly remember Gulshan trying in vain to lift me up as she screamed for help. She forgot about her own pain; all she cared about was saving me. Her calls for help, however, were being drowned out by my ear-splitting screams.

Those narrow streets with over a hundred people bore witness to my pain, but no one had the courage or the will to stop my attackers as they fled. I can't even blame them because I believe they were truly afraid. But ... afraid of what? The attackers? Afraid that they would also be attacked with acid? No. I think they were afraid of the system, the unspoken laws of our village. I think they had assumed that my attackers were powerful goons, and any attempt to stop them might mean a similar consequence for themselves. I don't know exactly.

It's possible that I am being too cynical. I have often wondered why no one came to my aid that day. Maybe no one knew what was really going on. Even I didn't know at the time that what they had attacked me with was acid.

What really shocked me was not that my attackers had got away, but the apathy of the onlookers. After the show was over, they turned their backs on me, the way I imagine they ignore injured stray animals every day. A stray dog, living or dead is of no value to most of us. They are beaten, attacked, and even killed if they dare to beg for food or eat from the trash or create a mess. My heart bleeds for them because I too was once like a wild, stray dog, howling for help that fell on disgusting, apathetic, wilfully deaf ears.

I begged my sister to kill me, to at least end the pain in some way. She could do neither. Instead, she held on to me tight as she looked around frantically, begging for help, for water, for someone to take me to the hospital.

On that narrow street, over a hundred witnesses stood motionless, watching from a safe distance. Not one person stepped forward. Humanity had ceased to exist.

My sister attempted to flag down a rickshaw, but the driver refused to take us to the hospital. Instead, he stepped off his rickshaw, casually leaned against a bicycle and, as he chewed on and spat out his paan by turns, as he asked the bystanders for updates on what was going on. My agony had become a source of gossip.

I was back to writhing on the ground and it took immense efforts to try and gain some control over my body. *Stop, Reshma, stop screaming, stand up, try to stand up. Stop screaming like this! You need to go to a hospital now or you will die.* I kept trying to talk sense to myself in my head, but I was still unable to get a grip. I noticed a few pairs of feet moving away and was later told people were giving me way as I snaked across the dirty, grime-filled road. The pain was so unbearable by now that I stopped talking to myself. I now prayed for instant death. I didn't even really understand what was happening to me. I had never even known what acid really was and Allah is my witness when I say that I could not work out for the life of me how I seemed to be burning in an invisible fire.

Soon, a man pulled up on a motorbike. Gulshan says he arrived within five minutes after the attack, but to me it felt like half an hour. That's the funny thing about time.

A few weeks later I began to play with time. I recalled what five minutes felt like while I lay burning on the hot tar road, and then compared it to what five minutes felt like while I watched TV, and thought about how that compared to me getting my skin debrided in the hospital for the same length of time. My favourite five minutes were the five extra ones I had started to ask for so I could sleep in a little longer, before the nurses came to change my dressing at the hospital in the mornings. Time is relative to the experience you're having. I hate time. It's a treacherous thing, one that makes you believe it's your friend before it comes sidelining your life like an enemy that's got you entrapped.

So, this one kind man among the crowd of hundred asked Firdoz and Afroz to help me sit behind him on his motorbike. As they lifted me off the ground, I could tell I was beginning to lose consciousness from the pain. But I focused the dregs of my energy on this man who was now my only ray of hope. And my brain told me I couldn't give up. Not yet.

With all my remaining courage and strength, I held on to him, wrapping my arms around his waist. I knew if I let go I would fall off the motorbike. I felt disoriented. Gulshan and this kind person had a quick conversation. My house and the closest hospital were both approximately ten minutes away. Since there was no room for Gulshan on the bike, she hailed an auto and rushed to the hospital. Firdoz and Afroz ran back home to inform my mother, while the kind stranger rushed me to Kesri Hospital.

By the time I reached the hospital, I had lost almost all my vision. The world looked blurry, the light seemed to have clouded over; I couldn't make out any shapes or details. Gulshan was already in the waiting area. I heard her gasp. Because of how hard I had been clinging to the man's back, his shirt had disintegrated from the acid on my clothes. His back had minor burns, which he said he would look into after getting home. He wished me luck on his way out.

I was rushed inside when I heard Gulshan arguing with a nurse. 'Please, help us. It's an emergency. Help this girl. She's my sister. She's been attacked with acid,' she pleaded as she supported me with her arms. She was helping me keep my own arms away from my body. They were burning and even a gentle touch hurt like a thousand piercing needles. Even the slightest stir of the air from people passing by caused me unimaginable agony.

'It's a hospital, everyone has an emergency. What makes her so special?' asked the nurse as she walked away nonchalantly to talk to some colleagues by the coffee machine. Gulshan asked me to stay where I was as she rushed off to look for someone else who might be able to help. That moment I felt a sudden chill that went deeper than the burns on my body. Had Gulshan also given up on me?

Thankfully, two minutes later she returned with a doctor. Then I heard my mother's voice and footsteps rushing towards us. 'Reshma, Reshma! Firdoz and Afroz came to see me. Why were they saying such terrible things? No, no, it can't be true!' My mother cried as she tried to hold my face and rub the acid off with her dupatta. But the cloth began to fall apart in her hands. She shrieked in horror and recoiled.

'Don't do that,' reprimanded the doctor. 'It'll only make the acid run deeper.'

My mother began to hyperventilate. I could hear her struggling to breathe through her tears. And then she fainted. The doctor rushed to her aid, sprinkled water on her face, and managed to bring her back to consciousness. She began to cry and apologize profusely. 'Look at your daughter. You will have time for tears later. Right now, she needs your help,' said the doctor as he made to leave. 'Stay strong, and I'm sorry I can't do anything before she registers as a patient.'

At that time, I was in no state to be concerned about my mother. I wanted her to get her act together and she did so after hearing the doctor's words. She took a deep breath. I heard her say a prayer under her breath and, with renewed strength, she rushed towards the receptionist.

Gulshan and Ammi spent a long time trying to get me admitted into the emergency ward or even just to get some first-aid care. But the hospital refused treatment.

I was still standing in the hallway; no one had offered me even a place to sit. Acid is a corrosive substance that continues to burn even hours after a person has been attacked with it. The only way to minimize the damage is to flush the affected area for hours with water. Water dilutes acid. No nurse or doctor made this suggestion.

By now my sister was urgently calling Mumbai, updating Riyaz, Aizaz and Abba. Nargis, who had got married just a year ago, in 2013, was also on her way to the hospital. She lived one hour away from where we did in Mau Aima. I later heard that my father had broken down when he was informed of the events. Aizaz, on the other hand, jumped into action and called my chacha for help booking *Tatkal* train tickets to Allahabad. Usually it takes weeks to get a confirmed seat on an Indian Railways train, but Chachu managed to find four tickets from Mumbai to Allahabad on the next available train for my father, my two brothers, and my cousin Shakeel, whom we lovingly call Chintu.

Meanwhile, my mother was navigating through an archaic, bureaucratic and painful system. The hospital wouldn't treat me as this was a criminal case, and I had to first file a police complaint. They refused to treat me without being given a copy of the First Information Report. An FIR, as we all know, is the first step to be taken after a crime is committed, whereby the police is provided an overview of the crime: who the victim is, where it took place, the nature of the crime, and so on. It is basically a first-witness account of the crime so criminal proceedings can begin. The law, however, states that in cases of severe injury to an individual, such as road accidents, acid attacks, and rape, the hospital must treat the victim first, without asking for a copy of the FIR.

In smaller villages and towns however, hospitals are unsure of the rules and, afraid of getting caught in bureaucratic criminal proceedings or blamed in any manner, they still insist on an FIR copy before tending to a victim.

What Kesri Hospital did was illegal. The Indian law states that an FIR must be filed immediately by anyone, a victim or a first-hand witness to the crime, and if it is not, due to some reason, the reason of delay must be stated at the time of filing. However, we were not aware of the rules back then, and as it turns out, neither was the hospital. So, I was to receive no treatment. My mother and Gulshan gave up arguing and rushed me to the police station, which was luckily just next door. As I stepped outside, the sun battered down on me and my pain intensified to a blinding agony. I began to wish for death again.

We rushed into the police station, where my mother pulled up a chair for me. The police officers entered one by one, casually. One of them sluggishly pulled out a sheet of paper and began writing down our account. As my sister recounted the event, he asked why I wasn't speaking. I kept my mouth shut because I knew if I opened it I would begin screaming again and not be able to stop myself. I didn't notice it at the time, but silent tears kept pouring out of my eyes, the tears of a living corpse. My eyes had swollen shut, my face was blistering with boils, and here was a police officer asking why I, the victim, wasn't answering his questions. At this point two more policemen walked in and asked Gulshan to repeat the story from the very beginning, more out of curiosity than anything else. It seemed they didn't want to miss out on any of the juicy details.

One of them asked why I had been attacked. Another wondered out loud if I was the one to blame. When Gulshan tried to explain that I was just seventeen, he responded with: 'So what? Seventeen-year-old girls are very clever nowadays. Who knows what she must have done to bring this on herself?' Yet another officer entered and began asking us the same questions. I was starting to feel angry, starting to understand why so many crimes go unreported in our country. *I* was being treated like the criminal, me, the victim of a horrific, nightmarish crime.

Gulshan began repeating the story all over again. Twenty minutes into it even the shadows began to disappear into the darkness. Panic started to grip me and I finally opened my mouth. Tears poured down my cheeks as I began to shriek.

'Stop this madness! Stop it! I'm dying, I can't see. My eyes, my eyes, my eyes! Kill me. KILL ME NOW!' I was ranting like a maniac.

I kept screaming as I clung on to my mother's arm till my nails dug into her skin. 'I can't see ... I'm going blind. Help me ... the pain ... help.'

A wave of nausea overpowered me. And then I threw up.

A quiet police officer who had been sitting at the next table jumped into action. 'Enough. Look at this poor child – she's just seventeen. We're taking her to a hospital. She can give her statement there. What if she loses her eyesight completely?' With that, he called for an ambulance to take me to the nearest hospital, after my sister and mother refused to take me back to Kesri Hospital because of how I had been treated there. Meanwhile, the police immediately gave us a copy of the written complaint since they feared the next hospital too would deny me treatment without that piece of paper. At that moment, that sheet held more value than my life. That piece of paper matters more to hospitals than saving the lives of the people for whom these facilities supposedly exist.

As an ambulance arrived from Bilak Hospital, my mother and sister jumped in with me. The police followed in their car. I began throwing up violently in the ambulance. When the human body goes into shock induced by pain, the nervous system reacts and nausea kicks in. My body was in so much distress that I gagged for half an hour. After a point I was just choking on nothing but excruciating pain.

We reached the hospital within ten minutes and, made nervous by the police's presence, the nurses and doctors rushed to my aid. Between wiping away my vomit and asking for the case history, the nurses rushed me to a quiet space, my family, the doctor, and the police at our heels. Blinding pain that still made death seem like a heavenly dream continued to cast shadows over my consciousness. It was as though I was living out a nightmare. I wasn't in my body; I had stepped out of my skin and could see my own mind being tormented. The thing I remember most vividly is the pain, the continuous vomiting, the blindness, and the raw panic.

The nurses helped me to a chair and I heard the doctor take in a quick, deep breath. I believe he was trying not to gasp out in horror. 'When did this happen?' he asked urgently. When the doctor discovered it had been over two hours, and I was yet to receive any medical care, let alone have my burns rinsed with water, he immediately ordered the nurses to fetch isotonic saline water and an anaesthetic injection.

'I can't believe no one used water on the burns,' he said and then went on to give those present a crash course on how to treat someone with acid or fire injuries. I can still recall some of it: 'Douse the injuries with fresh room-temperature water immediately. Do not use ice, do not use cold water. It will hurt more later if you use cold water because your skin temperature will drop significantly. That will only make things worse.'

My clothes were fused to my arms, my neck, my face, and my chest. Why wasn't he removing them? Somewhere above me I heard the doctor's voice, 'Remove any clothing and jewellery that has corroded to ensure it doesn't fuse with the skin. Do not attempt to take off clothing that has melted onto the person's skin, as that would only cause further harm by ripping off layers of skin along with the fabric. Let the doctors handle that.'

I know everyone listened with helplessness. Gulshan and my mother had found one more reason to blame themselves for my situation. Even today, Gulshan wonders why she hadn't thought of pouring water on me while I was burning, and my mother still blames herself for rubbing her dupatta on my face, causing more damage by spreading the acid. I prefer not to worry about it anymore. What's done is done.

The doctor cleaned my face with the isotonic saline water for half an hour. As he did he slowly snipped away the niqab from my face with a pair of scissors, damping the area with more saline water till it became easier for him to remove the cloth that was stuck in bits and pieces all over my face. Most of my niqab had disintegrated and melted away, but some of it was still fused to my skin. The pain was similar to someone stitching my face up with cloth in large knots and then ripping it off in one swift movement, pulling out chunks of my skin along with it. Every time the doctor snipped and tugged, I felt like I was being clawed.

To distract me from the pain he kept dispensing medical information. 'Regular water, if dirty, can cause severe infection and, I once read that over 90 per cent of burn victims who die, end up dying from preventable infections. Isotonic saline water, however, is a bacteria-free liquid with the same concentration as that of the body fluids like our blood and our tears.'

As the doctor continued to spray my face to dilute the acid and prevent it from seeping further into layers of my skin and my bones, I continued to cry. 'It's not helping, it's not helping. Make the pain stop.' The way he glorified the effects of water after a chemical burn, I truly believed my pain would now subside. But it didn't. At some point, he injected me with a painkiller, a mild, cheap one, I believe, since resources at such hospitals are rare and I didn't really find any relief.

After providing first aid for half an hour, the doctor turned to my mother and sister. 'You have to take her somewhere else. This hospital is not equipped to deal with such burns.'

I wondered why hospitals even existed.

7

A Dead, Rotting Rodent

SWAROOP RANI NEHRU HOSPITAL, a government hospital in Allahabad, is where I found myself next. By the time we reached all I wanted to do was sleep. What most people go a whole lifetime without enduring, I had endured in less than six hours. By now, I had stopped speaking completely.

Occasionally, Gulshan or Ammi would ask me how I was feeling. I wouldn't respond. When they asked if I was alright, I wouldn't even nod or shake my head. Quick whispers, panicked conversations, rushed calls were exchanged between Ammi and Gulshan. Abba was calling every ten minutes. At one point, Ammi got so flustered that she told him to stop calling because it was delaying them from getting me help. She told him to save his phone battery and asked him to bring money instead. She had none.

At Swaroop Rani Nehru Hospital, Gulshan rushed to the registration counter. The same old arduous sequence of events played out. Patient name, case history, identification, FIR ... At last, after an hour wasted at the counter, I was led to a ward and made to sit on a bed.

I stared at the floor blankly, quietly registering all the things I was being asked to do. I felt like I a life-sized doll. I couldn't even walk without someone holding my arm away from the rest of my body. My ability to understand words was drowning in my misery. I felt my deathwish return as I could no longer clearly see the world around me. When your mind is filled with shadows, you can still overcome the darkness if you have something to look forward to, but what did I have to live for now that I was going to be completely blind? All I could see were hazy colours and shapes. My vision had no clarity.

I didn't tell anyone this because I didn't think anyone would listen. I was an idealistic seventeen-year-old, but the last six hours had taught me to not put my faith in anything or anyone. My family had failed me, as had the hospitals and the police.

Gulshan tried to give me a glass of water to drink. My head was tilted backwards so I could take the water in; I didn't even have enough energy to hold my own head up. I couldn't part my lips. As Gulshan poured water into my mouth, it went trickling down the side of my face and down my neck. It reminded me of the acid, and I pushed away the glass violently.

'Reshma!' exclaimed my mother. I had never behaved like that with anyone, especially my eldest sister. I wanted to scream at my mother. Hurl abuses at her. Couldn't she see? I was no longer her daughter. I was no one at all and I could do whatever I wanted. I owed the world nothing after what it had done to me, and I took some pleasure in causing Ammi the pain I did in that moment. After everything that had happened, they wanted me to worry about my manners?

Pure rage swept through me. Humans are surely the worst kind of animals and I felt like I was one too. In disgust, I turned my head away from Ammi, only to feel a sharp, vengeful tug on the skin between my neck and my chin. The acid had fused them together.

Five minutes later, a doctor arrived. This was officially going to be the beginning of my treatment and I will always remember it as the start to a torturous journey which I had no option of abandoning, at least not if I wanted to survive. It started with them treating me like a person without a voice, thoughts, opinions, a soulless being without feelings.

Without asking me a single question, the doctor asked the nurse to hand him a pair of scissors. The previous doctor had simply removed the cloth that had fused with my face, but there was more stuck to my neck, chest, arms, back and stomach. Slowly, inch by inch, he sprayed water on my body as he began to snip away at the fabric that was still clinging to me. I watched the last of my decaying dignity fall off my body. I was naked from my chest now and the nurse tried to cover me up with a plain white cotton sheet. A strange thought occurred to me. In my country, the dead are always covered with white sheets. Maybe, hopefully, this was a sign.

Once the doctor was done, I heaved a sigh of relief. The attack itself had been a sudden onslaught of pain; however, afterwards, the pain had spread all over and the sharp throbbing of the first hours had subsided. Not for long though, I soon realized. Every time my scarred skin came in contact with something, anything, it throbbed violently. It was like being attacked with a fresh batch of acid.

I was too tired to ask for fresh clothes. But Gulshan and my mother were shocked at how unceremoniously I had been undressed. As a Muslim girl, I wore a niqab in accordance with our religious practices. But a doctor had stripped me of my clothes. Still, I felt more naked on the inside.

'Please, doctor, can you give Reshma some clothes?' my mother urged. The doctor explained that even a stray shred of clothing could lead to a severe infection, preventing my skin from healing, and possibly even leading to terrible consequences like death, as can happen in the most extreme cases.

'We don't have any clothes,' said the nurse, and the doctor didn't look pleased. 'Can you imagine – this is a hospital!' he said. Ammi wasn't happy with the state of affairs either. I frankly didn't care about being naked. I was still in shock.

'Can you at least give us some hospital gowns?' said Ammi.

'Out of stock,' came the unfeeling reply.

'We can't leave my sister here, lying naked like this. What are we supposed to do?' said Gulshan, panic rising in her voice. 'Her father and brothers are going to be arriving any minute now. They cannot see her like this. Their hearts will break.'

'There's a store right outside that sells clothes. Go buy something from there,' said the doctor as he asked me to open my mouth. I had blisters inside my mouth and my throat felt like it was being skinned every time I swallowed my saliva. When my attackers pushed me down to the ground, the acid had entered my mouth as I screamed.

The doctor sprayed my mouth and throat with water and kept asking me to open my mouth wider. I couldn't; it was as though even my jaws were fused together. Later, I found out that the corners of my lips had melted and got stuck together. While the doctor treated the sores in my mouth, Gulshan left to arrange some clothes for me.

Ammi and Gulshan didn't have much money with them – only around a hundred rupees – because the rest had been spent on the ambulance and medicines. Abba was bringing more cash, but until his arrival we needed to stretch out our funds. Gulshan was in tears by the time she reached the store. She asked to be shown the cheapest clothes, but the material was too rough; the doctor had specifically mentioned that rough cloth could lead to more sores and blisters.

The shopkeeper, a gentle old soul, read the pain on Gulshan's face and asked her what was wrong. On hearing her story, he pulled out the softest *malmal* suit he could find and gave it to her, free of charge. 'You can pay me back when your sister gets better,' he said. Gulshan returned with a soft cotton shalwar-kameez with a wide neck. For the second time that day she had witnessed human kindness.

Back at the hospital, Ammi and Gulshan spent a good half hour speaking about the fickleness of human nature. They dissected the circumstances of the day event by event, person by person, in order to better understand our circumstances and the state of things in general. 'India will never change,' said Gulshan.

'Even the police don't care,' said Ammi, but Gulshan was quick to point out that the system might fail us, but the common man is still kind and gentle at heart. My mother, overcome with emotions after hearing of the shopkeeper's kind gesture, could only nod in agreement.

I, still wrapped in the violent silence of my mind, thought to myself, if people can be so kind and gentle, why the hell did no one help me while I lay dying on the street? It wasn't the country, it wasn't the common man, and it wasn't the culture. It is just human nature to not care unless a tragedy affects you in some manner.

I suddenly realized that I hadn't spoken since I had cried for help at the police station. I decided to play a little game to see how long I could go on without speaking. Gulshan and Ammi were soon immersed in conversation, trying to work out the next steps of my recovery. They were not good company for me at the time. Slowly, I started to drift in and out of sleep. At some point a nurse arrived and hooked my arm up with an IV drip. She said something about burns dehydrating the body and I simply closed my eyes again. It hurt a bit as she inserted the needle, but soon I went off to sleep.

I certainly did not go to sleep because I was comfortable enough. It was the incredible agony that made me drift in and out of consciousness. I believe it was a means of escape from my new reality, and for the next one year, I slept more than I did anything else.

Without this newfound escape, I doubt I would have survived my ordeal. The only time I was ever at peace was when I was asleep.

A few hours later I woke up to someone howling. I kept my eyes closed. I didn't want anyone to know that I was awake so I wouldn't have to face a barrage of questions I couldn't really answer. A new patient was allotted a bed next to mine. It was her shrieks that had woken me up. She had doused herself in oil in an attempt to kill herself. A common enough occurrence in my country, although, the ground reality is that it is often not a suicide attempt, but an attempt at murder by in-laws, jealous husbands, or parents who believe their honour has somehow been ruined.

I felt someone touch my arm, someone who was sobbing quietly. 'Beta, what did they do to you? Why? Why you?' It was Abba. He wasn't really talking to me. He was talking to himself, or maybe to the jinns. I knew he thought they might have had something to do with the attack. He was probably trying to recall a million past mistakes, attempting to understand the gravity of these mistakes. Which mistake was it that had caused his daughter to suffer for his actions?

'Abba, don't talk like this, please, not in front of Reshma.' Aizaz, always the sensible one. His empathy was touching and we always said that his biggest downfall would be his deep concern.

'At least her face is not badly damaged. And we may be able to save her eyes,' said Ammi. I kept my eyes closed. Good, my face was not all gone. Good.

Little did we know that acid burns are traitorous companions. They hurt and burn in a manner that makes you give up on your will to live, and soon after they begin to show their softer side to the point where you're almost ready to forgive them. Like an abusive relationship, we all believed that the attack wasn't actually all that bad. Apart from the fact that I was in pain, my eyesight was compromised, and my skin was covered in blisters, we took consolation in the fact that I wasn't scarred beyond recognition. Not like those other girls in the news. Maybe the acid they had used on me was of a weaker concentration, and my family began to feel almost grateful that I would be alright. It could have been much worse. This was the beginning of an abusive relationship in which the acid made our spirits soar high and sink low, drowning us in a severe case of dreadfully false expectations.

Yes, my face looked more or less normal. For a week, somewhat. During that week my face was washed with saline water multiple times. My arms were covered in blue bruises from the unimaginable number of needles stuck in. I had thin veins, and it took several attempts to insert new IV needles. Sometimes my blood would flow backwards into the connecting wire.

For the one week I stayed at Swaroop Rani Nehru Hospital, I never saw a mirror. The nurses would hold me by both my arms and guide me to the bathroom so I could relieve myself. The bathroom had no mirrors either. I never took a bath because the motion of water trickling down my body would feel as though tiny, sharp teeth were gnawing at my skin. The nurses tried to give me gentle sponge baths, and I cried through those too. My skin was emitting a horrible acrid odour, and although my hair had burnt off there was a terrible smell that clung to my nose for days after. Burning hair has a distinctive stench that clings to your scalp for weeks. No matter how many sponge baths they gave me, the entire ward smelt like there was a dead, rotting rodent amongst us. Visitors would hold napkins over their noses. But I couldn't run away from myself, could I? Even today, any smell that triggers this memory, makes me want to throw up. Ammonia, charred meat, dead rodents ... they remind me of what I had once was been reduced to.

Every time I stepped out of bed I would feel dizzy. I could not eat at all, because my mouth was covered in blisters. They inserted a nasogastric tube through my nose and into my stomach. They would crush medicines and mix them with milk or fruit juice and gently send it down the tube. Often my stomach would bloat and cause me discomfort, a common side effect of eating through a nasogastric tube.

My one week at this hospital was our initiation into our new life. My family often asked the nurse whether they could speak to the doctor, to any doctor. But no doctor came by. The nurses would come, change my dressing, administer my medicines, and leave. My parents had to make inferences of their own. Would I need surgery? My skin was red, but it didn't look all that bad, did it? Perhaps the doctors weren't coming by because my case wasn't that severe.

By the end of the week my skin began erupting into painful blisters. My left eye began to shrivel into itself, but would not close completely. A small gap developed between my upper and lower eyelids and I lost my ability to blink or to open my eye wide. I lost vision in that eye, yet light was still filtering in, making it difficult to sleep.

At the end of the week a doctor dropped by. He clicked his tongue, aimed a flashlight at my face, and peered into my eyes. 'We won't be able to treat her here. Her eyes are badly damaged. Take her somewhere else,' he said as he walked off, indifferent to my parents' anxious questions.

Thankfully, the hospital was a government hospital. All we had to do was pay for the subsidized medicines I had utilized during the week.

8

Not Out of Danger Yet

I WAS ADMITTED TO a third hospital that week. Niyajuddin Hospital was also in Uttar Pradesh. I was provided a bed in the general ward and the sheets smelt musty. My mother asked for extra sheets, but was unceremoniously told to shut up as there were none available. She started arguing, saying there were blood stains on my sheets from goodness knows whose body, but Aizaz pulled her aside, apologizing profusely to the nurse.

'Ammi, please don't do this right now. It was very hard to get her admitted here and where will we take her if they throw us out? Let it go.' My mother bit her tongue then and on numerous occasions afterwards. Even as paying patients we were helpless within an underdeveloped and overpopulated medical system.

This is a sad, wretched country. Even a poor man believes he is part of the middle class when in fact he is so poor he is not even expected to pay taxes. The government hospitals are underfunded and resources are so scarce that a painkiller is considered to be a luxury for many. To put things into perspective, root canals are performed without administering local anaesthesia. They say it's too expensive and that the pain isn't really that bad. Women are slapped in the maternity wards when they scream too loudly. They bite their tongues till they bleed, lying on cold, hard metallic beds.

Our private hospitals are controlled strictly to the extent that people are petrified of doing their job. For example, many private hospitals refuse treatment to those that are supposed to receive free treatment under quotas set by the government. With such a large population, hospitals believe that they would go bankrupt if they treated every such person, even though private hospitals receive large economic concessions and are built on dirt-cheap government lands. Many pretend to not know the law and the ones that do pretend that the illness doesn't exist or is not severe enough.

In a nation where painkillers aren't easy to come by, pregnant women are slapped shut in delivery rooms, people are denied treatment because no beds are available, and doctors overcharge for patients who have already died.

The doctors at the previous hospital had not updated my family or me on what to expect during my recovery, and we had been optimistic for some time. During the one month I spent at Niyajuddin Hospital, we realized just how wrong we had been about the severity of my condition. Suddenly we found ourselves making hurried financial arrangements so we could be prepared for the upcoming medical bills.

This was the first time I began to sense economic ruin coming for my family. There would be numerous hushed phone calls between my father and his brother when Abba thought I was asleep: conversations on what property to sell, discussions about every single piece of jewellery my mother owned. Aizaz was looking for loans from cousins and my sister Nargis offered to call her husband for help. We had built a small, happy life for ourselves through generations of struggle, and all of that was unravelling because of the prohibitive medical expenses. With hospitals following a 'no payment, no treatment' policy, we had to create a buffer for any emergencies that might show themselves.

None of us had even heard of an acid attack until it happened to me. We believed that because my skin was initially just red with blisters slowly developing, it was perhaps on the path to healing. My eyes were of course a priority; however, my face, it seemed to us, would be alright.

Every morning the nurses would arrive at my bed and administer antibiotics through the IV line attached to my arm. They would then remove the previous day's bandages. By now the large blisters had begun to break, causing massive tears in my skin. Every time a bandage was removed with saline water I would howl in agony. The bandages would get stuck to the blisters, and removing them from my delicate skin would cause it to rip and bleed. The nurses would then begin the process of debriding old, unhealthy scar tissue.

This is my most painful memory from those days: a scary experience I had to endure for weeks. Burnt skin and tissue end up as dead and contaminated material on the burn wound, which can cause serious complications. Not only can they prevent timely healing, they can also cause severe, potentially fatal infections.

Every day the nurses would check on my wounds and prod me with sharp tools to measure the depth of the contaminated skin. They would then slowly graze at the dead skin, pulling off whatever they could with tweezers and forceps, making sure the skin was not being further damaged. A wet dressing was applied next, which was left to dry over the wound, and when it would be removed the next day, more dead skin and tissue would come off with it. The procedure was lengthy and painful. Sometimes a tug of the tweezer would make my whole body jerk with agony, and the pain would shoot up to my ears, and I would find myself clenching my teeth, biting the sides of my tongue. My body would shake violently and I would scream at them to stop, but the debriding process carried on.

'Stop shouting,' they would say. 'It's almost done,' but I knew better. Next, they would remove the dressing from my eyes and cover them with fresh bandages. Since my left eye would not shut properly, they had to keep it covered to prevent infection and also to stop light from streaming in. Without this cover, sleep was impossible. Every morning, after they removed the dressing from my eyes, they would wipe them with clean gauze. The blood and excretions from my forehead would continuously drip into my dressing, causing my eyes to be constantly moist. They would religiously give me some eye drop or the other at an hourly interval, in an attempt to keep my eyes clean.

My parents waited anxiously every evening for the doctor to come by for his rounds. He would come, check my dressings, and ask routine questions to ensure I had no infections.

'Do you have a fever? Are there white discharges coming from your wounds, or any foul smell when they change your bandages?' he would ask.

'No, doctor, nothing,' my mother would say since I never spoke.

She would then take over the conversation. 'Will she be able to see again?' she would ask persistently, refusing to accept his 'let's wait and see'. 'I really can't say,' he would maintain. Every morning he would take a sterile ear bud and pry my eyes open, flicking his torch into each eye. The vision in my right eye seemed to be good, however, I was nearly blind in my left eye. One day the doctor explained that because of the blood that was consistently dripping into my eyes, my left eye had become infected. I had lost my vision permanently and there was nothing they could do. He started to carefully monitor my right eye each day and advised me to continue with my eye drops. Over time the swelling would subside and I would be able to see normally with my right eye, I was told.

At the end of one week, the nurse removed the bandages from my forehead and gasped. My mother pulled up to my bedside immediately and began to hurl panicked questions at the nurse.

'What is this? Why is this happening?'

I was tired and all I wanted to do was sleep. But I kept my ears open, wondering what the commotion was about. What was going on? Apparently, the cartilage on my forehead had become exposed, all my skin had fallen off, and the bloody insides of my forehead were staring back at them.

The nurse ran to get the doctor and he arrived immediately.

'It's time to take her to Mumbai,' he said to my father. When my panic-stricken father and Aizaz tried to convince him to let me stay at the hospital, the doctor sat them down on the edge of my bed.

'Brother,' he said to my father kindly, 'this is a good thing. It means she is now ready for a skin graft. I can do that here, but the facilities available to monitor her eyesight are not good enough. She may lose her vision in both eyes permanently. We've waited to see if there is any sign of improvement, but there isn't. If we keep her here her right eye could also get damaged. It is vital to get a skin graft for her forehead so that it stops bleeding into her eyes. Please, take her to Mumbai. It's the best decision you could make for your daughter at the moment.'

'But her forehead … I can see her bones,' my mother said through her tears. Gulshan tried to get her to drink some water. 'She must be in so much pain, my poor child.'

I was in pain, and I was angry. I wished they would stop talking near me. I wanted to die, too, but more than anything else I wanted them to leave me alone. Didn't they understand that I may be blind, but I could still hear everything? I couldn't even see what I looked like.

'This was an acid attack,' said the doctor. 'Her face will never be the same again, but you can still try to do what you can for her eyes. Focus on making sure she can see again.'

After he left, my father asked the nurse what a skin graft was. None of us had ever heard of such a thing.

The next day, Aizaz had booked train tickets for all of us to return to Mumbai. The journey would be long and the doctor was afraid of the pain I would be in. He suggested we fly, but we couldn't afford the tickets. So, I was injected with a heavy sedative and my mother was handed half a dozen pills. 'Give her these. One painkiller every four hours, and a sleeping pill every six hours. Let her sleep through the journey. I don't know how else the poor child will survive this. A flight would have been the best.' My mother hung her head in sadness. There was no way we could buy a flight ticket.

I still had difficulty eating, and still had the nasogastric tube installed in my nose. The nurse had taught my mother how to administer medicines mixed with milk.

The journey to the train station was a nightmare. A taxi was called to drop us at the station entrance from where we had to take an overhead footbridge to our departure platform. As is usual with train stations in my country, this one, too, was crawling with thousands of people, each shoving and pushing one another. My family had surrounded me completely in a circle of safety, as they guided me by the arm. No one could bump into me and cause more injury. We found our seats by the train window. I was exhausted, in tears, and breathing heavily. I had not walked this much since my attack and I thought I would faint.

My mother administered my medicine and made my bed on the lower berth. The lower berth was supposed to accommodate three people, but my parents shared the berth across from me with my sisters and brothers just so I could sleep through the journey. They didn't sleep for a second; they could not, especially not after the phone call they received from the hospital.

While I was at the hospital, some of the nurses had become friendly with my family. Several of them sympathized with me, pained by the sufferings I had to endure at a young age through no fault of my own. They would sit and drink chai and gossip about the annoying family members of all the other patients they were looking after.

One of the nurses, Soni, had called to warn my mother of some danger to my family. Apparently, two women in long black abaayas had approached the nurses in both the general ward and the ICU, enquiring about a Reshma Qureshi. The nurses became suspicious because they knew I was already on my way to Mumbai with my entire family, and anyone else close to us would have known this. These two women also seemed to know our story, and their voices were unpleasant and harsh. One nurse tried to contact security. Another started to feel nervous while being questioned and started running in the opposite direction. The women followed her and tried to block her path. They grabbed the nurse and slapped her. As the nurse stepped back, she also tried to unveil one of her attackers. The attacker tripped over her abaaya and the nurse saw this as a perfect opportunity to remove the niqab. Behind the niqab was a man. The guards had arrived by then and forced the second assailant to remove the abaaya which revealed that both intruders were men in disguise. They quickly came up with an excuse, saying they had been concerned about me ever since reading about my attack in the local newspapers and that they just wanted to wish me good luck. They believed that it would be easier for women to meet me than strange men. They were asked to leave summarily.

The nurse had called my mother because she believed one of the men resembled Jamaluddin's nephew. She had seen his photos while we were at the hospital. But she could not convince security to hold the men since we were no longer patients at the hospital and the hospital did not wish to get into legal hassles.

We knew they had come back to kill me because we had filed an FIR against them. On hearing about their visit, Aizaz jumped into action. He called his close friends from the train and it was decided that while it was important to focus on my health, it was also very important to focus on the legal aspect of my case. While these men roamed free, we were all still in danger. The only way to get the police to act quicker would be to create a national media outcry. Aizaz and his friends sent press releases to every major national daily. My story would be all over the news through the next few weeks, until the police were pressured by the entire nation to take swifter action.

9

Survivors

I SLEPT THROUGH THE entire twenty-four-hour journey from Allahabad to Mumbai. Occasionally, my mother and sister would wake me up, lift my head to place it on their laps, and slowly make me drink milk or fruit juice. My medicines were diligently crushed into the liquids administered to me.

My mother woke me up at the station right before the one at which we were supposed to alight. With the copious sedatives I had been given, my family needed enough time to bring me back to my senses. I can't remember the name of the station where we were supposed to get off. I was tired and groggy. The Indian Railways are the busiest mode of transportation in India. My family rushed towards the doors with our luggage and stood there for a good fifteen minutes, waiting for the train to reach our destination. They didn't want to get held up by the disembarking crowd, not with me, not in the condition I was in. Five minutes before the train was supposed to make its stop, Aizaz and Abba came back for me.

'Move, please, make way,' they urged the passengers, opening up a safe passage for me. People stared as I started walking. I felt as if I was floating. I couldn't feel my legs and was being supported from both sides. Abba held my left arm and Aizaz the right.

The train slowly chugged into the station. A large group of people was waiting to board the train. But of course we couldn't expect them to let us alight first; it was going to be the usual grab-and-go chaos. But before the pushing and shoving could even begin, my father and brothers had jumped off the train and formed a human chain. They turned around to face the door of the train – where I was standing – completely blocking it off for anyone else. Behind me, my mother and sisters were doing the same to prevent people from leaving the train. I needed time and room to alight. 'She's hurt, don't push us, please, she's hurt,' screamed Aizaz to the people who were elbowing his back.

Some stepped back out of curiosity and looked at me transfixed. I felt uncomfortable, but at least the pushing had stopped. I could see people on their toes, heads bobbing to catch a glimpse of what the fuss was all about. Aizaz held out his hand and I grabbed it, literally falling into his arms. I had no sense of balance.

Ammi and my sisters were at my heels, and again a safe circle was created around me as we walked off the platform. We were expecting an arrival party. After my attack, my family had been barraged with concerned phone calls. Friends, cousins, family members, everyone had arrived to help us in whatever way possible. I heard loud cheers and voices to my right.

There stood a group of around forty people – I am not exaggerating. My family guided me towards the group where urgent hugs were exchanged; I was the only one who did not get any. No one wanted to hurt me again. The slightest human touch was agonizing. Now and then a gentle hand would brush against mine or graze my shoulder, as people greeted one another. I guess they didn't know what to say to me. If I had been in their place, I wouldn't have either. Sometimes, I caught the eye of an aunt or a friend, and noticed that they were averting their gaze, but I could catch their sympathetic vibes. No one spoke to me, and no words needed to be said. I had my own little army. Every direction I turned, I witnessed full-grown men wiping their tears. I knew many of my relatives present that day had given up their day's wages to be there for my family, for me.

I was tired and in pain, yet I felt relieved. Half the battles in India are won when people band in large numbers and with our solidarity, there was no doubt any hospital would deny me treatment. By now we had learnt it was best to have back-up; the plan was to get me admitted straight into a hospital in Mumbai. There was no time to go home, not after I had already lost one eye.

I was guided to the parking lot where a large rental van was waiting for me. I tried to get in, but it was too high. My mother and my maasi rushed in from the other side and pulled me inside, while Aizaz supported me up by holding my lower back. Earlier, I would always quickly scoot over to the middle. Now, just making it in through the door felt like progress.

My aunt quickly pulled out the sandwiches that she had so painstakingly wrapped in aluminium foil. They were passed around and everyone took one, except me. 'Reshma, beta, have a bite. It's your favourite,' said Ammi, as she extended a honey-and-cheese sandwich towards me. I didn't look at it. I maintained my unfaltering concentration on the view from my window.

A good two dozen autos, cars, and motorbikes surrounded us on our journey to the hospital. My guardian angels, I call them. The true strength of a person's character cannot be truly identified in times of joy, but rather in when adversity strikes. I didn't really appreciate the large number of supporters on the day of my arrival at the train station in Mumbai. But these people were the first in line to make phone calls to their connections, to donate blood when I needed it, and even pool in their savings to lend my father money, even though we had barely spoken to them in the past few months.

What surprised me was that some family members and friends, otherwise present at every wedding and festival, had conveniently only made the customary phone call to express concern. When financial or physical aid was requested, these same people stopped answering our calls.

However, today, the memory of the group escorting me to the hospital as a little battalion is one that is still fresh in my mind. I remember it as an image of beautiful friends riding in the sun, carrying hope for those who had almost lost every bit of it. My family was tired and crumpled, and without our support group, I don't know if we would have made it this far as victoriously as we had. There were struggles, of course, but our friends had lifted the burden off our shoulders and made it theirs without ever being asked to do so.

Soon, we arrived at the hospital. I waited downstairs in the seating area across from the registration booth. Even in the City of Dreams healthcare was just the same, with the same bureaucratic formalities. A copy of the complaint was handed over along with my medical history. The burns ward was overflowing with patients and I had to wait for the authorities to organize a bed for me. I later found out that a patient had to be forcibly removed to make room for me. Beds were given on priority, and my case warranted priority. I didn't know where that patient went, but I could only guess – she would have been given a spot on the floor.

After registration, my family waited in the reception area while Ammi and Aizaz escorted me to the burns ward. We entered the elevator and immediately people stared. I was grotesque, even by hospital inmate standards. Where did I belong if not there, I wanted to ask, but I hadn't spoken in weeks, even though my mind was bleeding out words that were clotting in my mouth.

As we reached the burns ward, a door was opened for us that led into a narrow corridor. I promise I could smell death. Many people I saw there had their mouths covered with dupattas or handkerchiefs. Another door opened at the end of the corridor, leading to a large room with around thirty beds lined up against the walls to my left and right. These beds were all linked to machines that overwhelmed me with their strange otherworldly sounds. My heart started to throb with fear. The first thing I remember are the screams that went ignored. The second: people lying helpless on the floor.

I forced myself to focus on my breathing. It was an apocalypse; there was literally blood on the walls. My slippers were sticking to the floor and I looked down to find red stains that had remained after the floor had been half-heartedly mopped with what smelled like Dettol. But the smell of Dettol couldn't mask the smell of death. I wanted to throw up. No wonder people had covered their mouths. That room was the closest I had ever been to death. Patients with burns on their arms and legs were resting against the walls, and often we would accidentally step on their loose, bloody bandages. Everywhere I looked there was a patient begging for a nurse's attention, for painkillers, for water. The nurses just walked on by, stepping over limbs.

What I saw on the beds still gives me nightmares. Completely burnt, deformed, grotesque bodies with large tent-like coverings over them. A white sheet covered these tents, because the bodies underneath were naked. I saw a woman sitting up on her bed, her chest completely bare, but she didn't seem to be bothered. She was looking at the people passing by with blank, unblinking eyes. Tears poured down her face as we walked by her bed, and her eyes following me eerily. I stared back; I simply couldn't look away. Even though she was looking right at me it seemed as though she wasn't really in her body. I suppose she had done all her screaming, and these silent tears were an admission of defeat. Her neck was tilted towards her right shoulder. She didn't even have the energy to hold her head up straight. Her arms lay limp by her side, her palms open skywards. The tears never stopped.

When the nurse pointed at my bed I felt pure rage. I was in so much pain and I could not believe these were the best facilities available for me. The deathwish reared its head again. There were no curtains to block my harrowing surroundings either. Even if curtains could be found, I still needed soundproof walls to prevent the screams from filtering in. I felt disoriented, my eyes scanning the room, my breathing getting heavier and heavier. Even as I tried to stare at a blank sheet, botched, burnt faces went skirting past my mind, as my imagination rendered them all the more haunting. A blood-curdling howl erupted on my right, a loud animal-like shriek that reminded me of my own attack.

I broke down. I grabbed Aizaz by his arm and made my first demand since my attack. 'Take me away from here, Bhai. I will not stay here, I will not. I will die; I will kill myself if I have to. I will burn myself to ashes a thousand times over, but this pain will consume me from within. I will lose my will to live. Look at these people, they're already dead. Please don't leave me here.'

'Reshma, beta, calm down,' said Ammi, stroking my arm. 'Reshma, beta, this is the only burns ward around. They are all the same, no matter where you go.'

I fell on the floor and grabbed my brother's legs, begging him for mercy. This was the only burns ward they had and the nurses couldn't even change the bloodied sheets for a new patient? Hysteria had taken over me and in any humane setting I believe strangers would have come to our aid or at least stopped to find out what was going on. But considering how that ward drove everyone insane, no kind stranger stopped by. Instead, I saw two nurses snigger over our misery.

Ugly, disconcerting thoughts began to invade my mind. For the first time a seed of doubt was planted in my head, one born of the most desperate kind of helplessness. My own sister's husband had attacked me with acid. He had actually wanted to attack my sister, his own wife. Could we trust anyone in this world? I had to suffer this pain alone and then die alone as well. Maybe my family too would leave me stranded with my horror and simply walk away. Maybe I had been enough of a burden already. My brother's words did not help. What happened next is one of my uglier memories.

'Reshma, please, this is the best we can do,' said Aizaz. 'You must be strong. For us. We need you to be strong.' I must be strong for them? I was the strongest out of all of them. If they had been in my position they would have tried to kill themselves already. Not that the thought hadn't crossed my mind, but at least I hadn't acted upon it. I wanted to say this out loud, but I didn't. Instead, I decided to blame them for my situation, hoping that their guilt would convince them to find a better alternative for me.

'I will not stay here,' I screamed at Ammi. 'It's because of you that I'm here in the first place. Abba and your decisions have ruined my life. I'm paying for your stupid decisions because you couldn't even find a decent husband for your daughter.' That statement, spat out in a fit of rage, would go on to haunt my family and myself for a long, long time.

Words are dangerous, and very powerful indeed. Scars caused by words create lesions that sometimes don't heal in an entire lifetime.

The venomous words I spoke that day can never be taken back. The horror and guilt I had unleashed in the minds of those I loved can never be undone. For years they have treated me with love, as they do even now. For years I have tested their boundaries, driving them to lash out at me and scream at me like they used to. But they won't do it anymore. I wish I had never insinuated that my family's decisions had led to my attack. For their sake and for mine. I stopped trusting them, because I believed that they were always trying to please me. I realized that a few poisonous words said in anger had forever altered the way my family treated me. Their mannerisms towards me were always controlled by a sense of guilt.

That day, in the burns ward, I was nothing short of a monster. I was so afraid of my surroundings that I decided to emotionally manipulate my family to get away from them. In a fit of despair, I began to hurl fierce allegations that I didn't really mean. Somewhere in my mind I knew exactly what strings I had to pull and that, mixed with my anger, made me delusional. 'It's your fault that I'm here, you hear me?' I repeated. 'I'm just seventeen. I was twelve when Gulshan married that man. Why did he attack *me*? You should have seen this coming. How could you not see that Gulshan was being abused? You're just going to leave me here in this hell while you sit outside drinking hot tea, pretending to be worried. At least the neighbours won't think badly of you when they see that you are in pain.'

This was the first time since the attack that I had released such intense emotions and it must have been a confusing and painful sight for my family. Ammi came closer to me and held both my arms. 'Reshma, beta, please don't cry,' she said. She was crying herself. 'Beta, we don't want to leave you here. This is the best burns ward in Mumbai. All we want is for you to get better. I pray to Allah every day so he would take away my face and give you back your eyesight. I ask him why it wasn't me. Please forgive me, Reshma.' She broke down and what I did next is where my regret stems from.

'Good. Even I wonder why he wouldn't do that. Get away from me.' I pushed Ammi away and walked out of the room with a renewed sense of energy I had not felt for weeks.

'Let her go,' I heard Aizaz sigh in defeat. Ammi and Aizaz followed me outside in silence. We stepped into the elevator. I pressed the button for the ground floor, where I joined the rest of my family, to whom I offered no explanation of the events that had just unfolded.

Gulshan walked over and quietly whispered into my ear, 'Reshma, what happened?' I shook my head. I had withdrawn into myself again.

I was deeply embarrassed by my own outburst and wanted nothing more than to ask for an apology, but I couldn't bring myself to do it. Sometimes, an apology isn't commensurate with the graveness of one's mistake. I find it's easier to apologize for smaller slights, but the larger faults, those are forgiven over time, and not because you have asked for it, but because you have proved yourself worthy.

Aizaz was kind enough to take the blame and Ammi was still reeling from the shock caused by my words. 'That ward was unacceptable,' said Aizaz. 'Reshma won't be comfortable there, and she definitely won't get any better. Infection is a big risk and we can't let her stay there.'

'Aizaz,' said Abba in his sternest voice. 'Do you want your sister to get better? What other option do we have? Ignore your whims and fancies. She seems fine. Stop putting your stupid ideas in her head.' And there it was again, conversations that forgot about my presence. I stared at the floor. Gulshan held my hand. Abba hadn't even really seen the ward. I wanted him to shut up before voicing an opinion about something he hadn't even seen for himself.

'What the hell are we supposed to do now?' asked Abba.

And then one of our friends championed Aizaz's cause. 'Don't worry, Bhaijaan,' he said. 'I know a local politician. Why don't you all wait here a while and I will see what I can do. Reena, bring them some chai and *khana*,' he said to his wife as he walked off to make some phone calls. Again, the people who had come to pick us up from the train station surrounded us, distracted us from our thoughts, and made sure no argument would break out between Abba and Aizaz. In their presence, Abba calmed down. I pretended to doze off in my chair so no one would talk to me.

About forty-five minutes later, a man arrived. A man named Gautam Sharma. He was a politician in our district – Chembur. He wasn't rich, nor was he powerful, but he was a man of morals and committed towards helping the members of his constituency. He promised my father that I would receive a private, air-conditioned room, and on that note he began the harrowing process of championing my cause. Aizaz accompanied him, armed with my full medical history. The process took over two hours.

Mr Sharma first went to the registration counter and asked for a private room for me. The woman at the desk refused on the principle that I was a burns patient and that I had already been accommodated in the burns ward. If I didn't like what was available, I could go wherever I wished. Mr Sharma explained my situation, how severe my injuries were, and how I was just a seventeen-year-old who could not bear the palpable trauma in that ward. The nurse refused, so Mr Sharma requested to see someone higher up. His request was denied, but when he mentioned he was a local politician his request was immediately granted. It was like magic.

Mr Sharma got us an audience with the medical superintendent of the hospital. This gentleman was a kind man. Mr Sharma explained my predicament with Aizaz's support, and showed him my before-and-after photographs.

I was yet to see my reflection in a mirror, or any photographs of my post-attack face. So, naturally, I didn't know they were used as an influencing factor, but they got me a private air-conditioned room at twenty-five per cent of the usual price. I found out about the photographs years later, when Riyaz brought it up while talking to someone about the kindness Mr Sharma had extended towards our family.

The superintendent was deeply unsettled by the story and immediately ordered his juniors to ensure that I was made comfortable, and that a discounted surgical and medical care estimate sheet be provided to my family in order for us to make the necessary financial arrangements at the time of my discharge. An advance was requested, which all three of my father's younger brothers footed for us. He told Abba that his niece's recovery was of utmost importance and Abba could pay them back at a suitable time. I believe that the loan, which amounts to several lakhs, is yet to be fully repaid.

Within the next hour I moved into my private room in a ward that oversaw the severest of cases at the hospital. I entered the ward and walked down a corridor flanked by doors leading to private rooms on either side. These rooms held patients with terrible cases that would be talked about in hushed voices. These cases were not severe because of the medical situation itself, but because of what had happened to them. The patients were all women, abused women. The most common case was that of women being set on fire by their in-laws or husbands. They always make me wonder about Gulshan's possible fate had she not left Jamaluddin's house.

Then there were women who had been forced to perform violent, at-home abortions after being forced to undergo illegal sex determination. These were procedures that the government has banned in order to prevent female infanticide. As we all know, legally, parents can only learn the sex of their child after its birth.

We heard of one woman who was being treated courtesy of an NGO fighting for the cause of women's rights. No one came to visit her and she rarely spoke. Occasionally a volunteer from the NGO would come, get an update, and leave once all practical matters were taken care of. That patient had a psychologist, though. No one knows what she said to her therapist, or if she even spoke at all. This young woman had been forced to go through a sex-determination procedure, and when her husband and father-in-law discovered that the foetus was female, they beat her mercilessly. Her fault was that she was pregnant with a girl child.

Some people at the hospital said that she had apparently tried to run to the neighbours for help, but her mother-in-law and sister-in-law caught her, tied her to the foot of the bed and gagged her mouth shut. That night they beat her till she fainted. When she regained consciousness, they beat her again till she passed out. In time she realized the best bet was to feign unconsciousness, but when she had kept up the pretence for too long they shoved her head in a bucket of water until she gasped for air. They then beat her again. This cycle continued till six or seven in the morning, after which her husband and his father began to jump on her stomach till she started bleeding. That's the story of how this young woman's unborn girl child was murdered by her own father. I believe in abortions, but this level of depravity is not an abortion. It's the murder of humanity itself.

When my sisters and I heard this story, we were heartbroken. I didn't comment on the situation at all because I was facing demons of my own. I wondered if I should try and speak to her, but never acted upon that instinct. What help could I possibly have offered her? But I regret this hesitation. Today, I wish to reach out and speak to every such woman and tell her that there is hope, and that even if they can't see it, I will fight for their future and diminish their pain the same way people did for me in the years following my attack.

There were also cases of rape. All rape survivors in that ward had suffered unspeakable brutalities. I got to know them during my stay, and dwelling on their stories will consume me with depression. I don't believe I had ever seen a rape victim before I entered that ward at the age of seventeen. But then, how can I be so sure?

I live in India. My capital, New Delhi, is infamously known as the rape capital of my country. After 16 December 2012, the entire world learned about a twenty-three-year-old woman who was brutally gang raped in a moving bus while returning home from the cinema. Jyoti Singh, a physiotherapy intern, boarded the bus at 9:30 p.m. with a male friend. There were six other men, including the driver. All drunk. During the course of that night they beat her friend and knocked him unconscious. Then they proceeded to destroy her life.

They moved her to the back of the bus where they took turns to rape her repeatedly. She tried to fight them off, biting and kicking helplessly. One of her attackers, a juvenile who sent to a correction home and has now been released, inserted a rusted metal rod into her vagina. When they were done with her, they threw her and her friend out, naked, on the street.

A passer-by rushed them to the hospital and Jyoti was put on life support. One of the accused admitted to seeing some red rope-like material coming out of her body as the juvenile pulled out the metal rod with which he had assaulted her. That rope was her intestines. She had none left in her when she died; all of it had to be removed. Jyoti suffered violent damage to her intestines, uterus and genitals.

The nation called her 'Nirbhaya', the fearless. We erupted with rage at the crippled governance of our nation and massive, nationwide protests took place in the days to come. On 29 December 2012, Jyoti died in a hospital in Singapore where she had been later taken for treatment. The government, for the first time, had no choice but to listen to us. Thousands of protestors clashed with the police and Rapid Action Force units had to be deployed. The protestors were met with water cannons, lathi charges and tear gas. New Delhi came to a halt. On 21 December, a peaceful protest took place at India Gate, the heart of the capital. Metro stations were shut, and the police cordoned off roads in order to ensure the crowds wouldn't get out of hand. This was the final straw. A war was being waged. A much-needed war for women, for one half of our population.

In response to the case, fast-track courts were set up, new laws discussed, to ensure swift justice in cases of rape. However, it still took five years for the verdict to be released in the Nirbhaya case. While the accused were sentenced to death, the juvenile who caused her death is now twenty-three, rehabilitated by an NGO, and working under a false identity in southern India. He was seventeen when he raped her. I wonder how much wiser a person can get in a few more months, how they can become an 'adult' overnight. The lawyer defending the rapists said that if his daughter had been out so late at night, he would have personally taken her to a farmhouse and burnt her alive. We knew change was coming when the nation retaliated to his comment with an overpowering rage.

However, nothing much has changed. Incidents of rape and acid attacks are on the rise. Early in 2018, an eight-month-old baby was raped by her twenty-seven-year-old cousin. She was bleeding profusely from her genitals and was put on life support. This man claimed in his defence that he thought of the infant as an adult. Our newspapers are flooded with such horrific stories every single day. The 'normal' cases, which don't involve victims being raped with rods or being put on life support, often don't even make it to the papers.

As I said, I believed I had never met a rape survivor before I set foot in that hospital ward. In a nation where millions of women are victims of this atrocity I probably must have met some without knowing it. However, owing to victim-blaming and the growing tribe of 'meninists', it is safe to assume that women often remain silent, hiding behind a shame that is not theirs to bear in the first place.

I was in that hospital room for fifteen days. Multiple women came and left. All of them raped, burnt, or tortured. I also realized they were granted these rooms under special circumstances. They were all poor, incapable of funding such expensive medical treatment. I shudder to think where I might have been had it not been for the kindness of Mr Sharma.

In India, the word 'politician' is automatically associated with corruption and an unhealthy fondness for power. But in a country of more than a billion people, which also happens to be the largest democracy in the world, we also have thousands of Gautam Sharmas. These are local neighbourhood political leaders who never make it as Members of Parliament or Ministers of State. I believe the real change in our nation is happening because of people like Gautam Sharma. Not just him, but also young, idealistic activists and people who dedicate their lives to making a difference at the grassroots. They cover potholes during the rainy season, petition to end over-the-counter sale of acid, ensure that the poor are able to avail the medical subsidy quotas the government has set in place, and hold the top leaders accountable for their inadequacies.

Our judiciary system is as strong in laying down commendable laws as our top politicians are weak when it comes to ensuring tools to implement them. One would think that in the worst-case medical scenario, the health minister would be the one to take important decisions. However, in February 2015, C. Laxma Reddy, health minister for the state of Telengana, walked past a dying man who was begging for help outside a hospital where he was on an inspection visit. I don't know if there was a follow-up story, but I know in all probability he died. He was lying on the ground, unable to pull himself up, and going by how wretchedly thin he looked in the photographs that flooded the papers, he probably weighed less than me. If the health minister did not stop to question why this dying man was left unattended on the dirty streets, I wonder who else will. Don't we lead by example?

And then I think about people like Gautam Sharma, and the numerous social workers and human rights activists that have been a part of my journey since my attack. Had that man known someone like them, he may still be alive. Our laws are strong and just, but their implementation is nothing short of an embarrassment. Change is occurring, but it takes time and often comes from the least expected direction. While our political leaders continue to sing praises of our laws, the laws are doing less to protect our people than activists on the ground. Change in India is a trickle-up effect, and I wish our top leaders could learn from some of the people I know.

10

Future Plans

BY THE TIME I was admitted to the private air-conditioned room in the hospital in Mumbai, I had already lost all vision in my left eye. My eyeball shrank into my eye socket, creating a shallow dent. Thankfully, the swelling in my right eye had subsided and my vision was intact. I could blink and the eye seemed to function normally.

The doctors at the hospital consulted with their teams to come up with the best solution to prevent my right eye from suffering the same fate as the other. I was advised to keep my right eye covered with fresh, clean bandages at all times and given numerous medications so I the good eye would have further clarity. The doctors decided to perform two surgeries subsequently. The first, a major procedure, was to place a skin graft over my entire forehead to stop the discharge and cover the exposed cartilage.

The second surgery involved a small graft on my left eyelid. The bone and cartilage on my left eyelid – right below where my eyebrow used to be – were also exposed. My eyebrows and eyelashes had burnt into nothingness during the attack.

When I learnt about this, I remembered an incident from my mid-teens. When I turned fifteen, I left my tomboy ways behind and began to embrace my feminine side, even fall in love with it. I loved putting on make-up and buying pretty jewellery. I remember this one peculiar tragedy that makes me laugh at my naivety. Like so many girls my age, at sixteen I had gone to a local beauty parlour to get my threading done for the first time. I winced in pain as the parlour woman plucked my upper lip hair with a piece of thread. But getting my eyebrows shaped took the pain to a different height altogether. I sat there, my eye tightly shut. I felt a sharp nick and let go of my grip on my forehead. The lady gasped. She had lost control because I had opened my eye suddenly. When I saw my reflection in the mirror, I cried out loud. Half my eyebrow had been sliced off! I ran home in distress and screamed at Nargis for recommending such a stupid place. This was my first eyebrow threading try-out and I had come home with half an eyebrow! What would people say?

I was so embarrassed that I declared I would be fully veiled in a niqab and abaaya, from head to toe, until my eyebrow grew back. My brother Aizaz had always disliked the hijab and had tried to convince me to stop wearing it on numerous occasions. The hijab is a headscarf Muslim women wear to cover their head, ears, and neck. The niqab, however, is a full face covering that only has slits for the eyes so one can see through the veil. When he heard my plan to cover my face with the niqab, he became upset. 'Reshma, stop it. We live in India. You'll look like an idiot. You shouldn't even be wearing the hijab. It's an eyebrow, for Allah's sake! It'll grow back!'

I was crying and at that point my half-eyebrow was the biggest problem in my life. I never wore the niqab because Ammi bought me kajal and showed me how to draw the perfect eyebrow till the real one grew back.

However, just about a year later, here I was with no hair, no left eye, no eyelashes, and no eyebrows at all. This thought plagued me with despair. I began blaming myself for my destiny. Perhaps I, too, was at fault. Jamaluddin probably knew how concerned I was with beauty and realized it would be the ultimate act of revenge to take mine away.

And now, because of that vile man, I was going to have the first surgery of my life at this hospital. Visitors came the night before and asked if I was scared. I shook my head. I wasn't trying to be brave, nor was I comforted by the thought of general anaesthesia and painkillers. It's just that I'd suffered enough to know that a surgery is nothing. Billions of people go through surgeries, but it's only thousands who have survived acid attacks. I wanted everyone to stop talking to me. Actually, that's not right. It was more like they were talking at me … as usual.

I said nothing. On the night before my surgery, a team of interns arrived with my nurse. They checked my vitals and told me to not drink or eat anything for the next twelve hours. I was also told that the two procedures would be taking place simultaneously because I would require numerous surgeries in the future. General anaesthesia is extremely harmful for the body, and it would be best to minimize its use considering the number of times I would have to go under the knife. I nodded in agreement, as did everyone in my family. It's not as though we had any opinions. Most of us hadn't even graduated high school. What would we know about all these medical technicalities?

The nurse then explained that in order to perform the graft they would take some skin from my groin region, the most suitable skin to adapt to my face. This was one of those rare moments in which I spoke. 'No,' I said. 'No, no, no. Can you imagine the pain? I won't even be able to walk!'

For once, Ammi agreed to stand by me. 'Come up with an alternative. We'll take the risk. She can't suffer any more.' The nurse and interns tried to convince us to no avail. At the end, it was decided that the graft would come from my inner thigh.

They checked my vitals again on the morning of the surgery. A nurse arrived with cotton and nail-polish remover – the surgical team would need to check my nails during the surgery to ensure there was no problem in blood flow to my extremities. I looked down at my toes in surprise. Nail paint? I used to wear nail paint? It seemed so frivolous.

I had forgotten about the trivial things with which normal girls concern themselves. I also felt bad that the poor nurse had to remove nail paint from my feet which were probably ugly and disgusting. I wondered how bad I really looked. Why had no one shown me a mirror yet? I vowed to never wear nail polish again. That, of course, would depend on if I ever left the hospital.

Suddenly, I felt a deep sorrow settle over my chest. Taking a breath seemed strenuous. I realized I had no future. If I did leave the hospital, what exactly would my life be like? Would I be able to just go back to wearing nail paint as if nothing had ever happened? No one would want to marry me, I wouldn't be able to complete my education, and I would never have a job. Was I supposed to sit behind closed doors until my dying day? This was the first time I felt a deep jealousy for the regular girls. Why did they have the privilege of going to college, skipping classes, watching movies, having crushes, and complaining about their weight? I hadn't even seen any mountains yet, or snow. I hadn't even finished school. My whole future was an endless black ocean. Earlier, when I would feel unsure about my future, I would let my imagination run wild, and it would conjure all kinds of optimistic, entertaining scenarios. Now, along with my vision, my hair, my dignity, I had been stripped of this imagination as well.

No matter how hard I tried to imagine a future, the most pleasant outcome was death. I began to fantasize about my funeral. My idea of romance was how much people would cry at my funeral. I wondered who would attend and who would think of me for years to come. From then on, for months after, I imagined my own death. In one scenario, I would die during surgery. In another, I would commit suicide, a gunshot through the nape of my neck or by slitting my wrists. I never imagined setting myself on fire, though. In another scenario, I would attack Jamaluddin with acid and he would kill me in retaliation. This was my favourite scenario.

I was jerked out of my thoughts once I entered the operation theatre. After the surgery, I woke up feeling nauseous.

The pain was sharp, especially in my thigh, from where they had cut layers of skin to graft on my forehead. I was screaming for painkillers, but was denied any. I felt disoriented because the drugs were still in my system. Our government controls painkillers because they fear its misuse. Morphine wasn't available at the time, so I was given something much weaker. I remember that a year or so later I read about a case where a man in the US was caught in a fire. He suffered forty per cent burns and was put in an induced coma. Whereas in India, patients with even eighty to ninety per cent burns are denied morphine. The difference is crippling.

When I was discharged from the hospital, the doctors recommended that I should stay in an air-conditioned room since the humidity in Mumbai could cause my graft to sweat, leading to complications.

Ammi's sister had a small home, but it had an air conditioner. I was to stay there till the doctors cleared me to go back to my own home. My family dropped me off at Maasi's house. We had lunch and then they left saying they would be back the next morning. I took a nap after lunch and, when I woke up, I went to use the bathroom.

It was while washing my hands that I looked up at the mirror. I saw myself for the first time since that attack. It had been two months. I was transfixed at my own reflection, especially my deformed eyes. I panicked.

I knew that my face was damaged, but this face in the mirror wasn't mine. It looked like a strange creature that could not have been me.

All my features had melted off, my left eye had nearly disappeared, my lower lips looked like a melted candle, drooping and fused with my jaw, my teeth exposed permanently. My cheeks were coarse and hard and had none of their earlier vitality, bloodied scars pock-marked what used to be smooth skin. My forehead was covered in bandages, yellowed with medication and pus. My skin was red and bloodied and my nose had exposed cartilage. I looked as though I had risen from the dead. Tears sprang to my eyes. I can never translate my shock into words. No wonder my little nephew had begun to cry on seeing me. I thought it was because he was worried for me, but now I knew why – I looked scary.

I wished for death again. I couldn't go out in public like this. People would think I was diseased or, worse, a walking curse. I don't know what overcame me next, but I quickly wrapped a scarf around my face and ran out of the house, towards my own chawl. I couldn't live with my maasi. Not if I looked like this. No one deserved to be burdened by my monstrosity. No one except my family, who was responsible for this tragedy.

I jumped into an auto and directed the driver to my house. I rushed upstairs to our one-room excuse of a home. I don't remember what I did when I got home, or what thoughts were running through my mind. It's still a gap in my memory. Next thing I knew, Ammi and Aizaz found me in the kitchen, a butcher's knife in my hand. I was examining it carefully, tracing the edges of the knife with my finger. That's when Ammi started to scream.

'Reshma, what are you doing?' she said, as she lunged towards me. Aizaz pulled her back. 'Ammi, no. You'll scare her,' he said.

'Reshma. Reshma, listen to me,' he said. 'Please give me the knife.'

'I want to die,' I said.

'Not today, Reshma. Look at Ammi. Think of Abba. Abba will die without you. He is in so much pain. If we could, we would all take your pain and multiply it a thousand times over for ourselves. We pray to Allah to take away years of our lives to give you some happiness in yours. We will all die without you, Reshma.' I shook my head, sobbing as I fell to the ground. 'And think about Jamaluddin. Don't you want to see him in prison, or better yet, hung for his crimes? Reshma, without you, the case will never go to court. Saufi will never be found.'

The second I heard Saufi's name I got a grip on myself and put the knife down. I could not allow another innocent life to suffer that cruel man's criminal wrath. Especially not my nephew's. No one had seen him since the day Jamaluddin kidnapped him from school, since the day he was dragged back inside when my parents had gone over to their house.

I owed Gulshan as well. She had suffered years of his abuse and, due to the severity of my burns, she had ignored the damage to her own arm. No one had even looked at her arm again. I wondered if she was getting it treated at all. It was Saufi, Gulshan, Abba, Ammi, and my quest for justice that stopped me from taking my life that day.

Ammi handed the knife to Aizaz who quickly put it away in a cupboard and locked it. He put the key in his pocket. Ammi consoled me as I sat on the floor crying. She gave me water and I took a few sips. I was exhausted. I went to lie down at my usual spot on the floor, but Ammi stopped me. 'Sleep on the bed; we'll all sleep on the floor.'

While I slept, Aizaz and Ammi locked away every sharp object they could find. When I made it clear that I would not go back to my aunt's house, Abba and Aizaz quickly went to the market to buy an air conditioner. They found an electrician and had it installed the very same day. I knew the cost would be heavy to bear, but my family was willing to sell their soul for my comfort. I slept well that night. We had never had an AC before.

The next morning I woke up to the sound of guests. Some relatives and friends had come to visit me. I sat up and stared at them, without offering a hello or a smile. I hadn't had a proper conversation with anyone since my attack. They had heard about my suicide attempt. Ammi thought that inviting them over would distract me from my thoughts.

The women clicked their tongues and tried to talk to me. 'Reshma beta, *kaisi ho*?' asked an aunt. I didn't respond. I just kept my eyes fixed the wall. '*Bechari*, she must be tired,' said another, attempting to make sense of my slight.

'*Haan*, look at her,' said another. 'You're a very brave girl indeed. I don't know how you've been so strong.' She came and swept her hand over my now bald head. The sensation of her hand on my scalp made that now-familiar rage explode through my body. I started to tremble and clenched my teeth. I hated these unnecessary visitors.

'She is very brave. She's a little tigress,' said Ammi as she smiled at the visitor.

This was my breaking point. Ever since my attack I had harboured a million confused feelings. And even when I wanted nothing more than to be left alone, people always surrounded me. These same people then went on to talk about my attack and injuries as though I wasn't even there. I was the victim and they continued to make me relive the memory I was trying so hard to fight and forget. They would then talk about the pain

I must be in as if they understood even a fraction of it. What I hated most, though, was how they would assume how I felt. '*Sab theek ho jayega*, everything will be okay,' some of them would say. I never spoke to any of them, yet they managed to invalidate my deepest pain. I would also hear things like: 'Poor girl, she must be worried. Who will marry her now?' I wanted to claw the tongues out of these women's mouths. Yes, I was worried. I was worried that I was going to live in a living hell until my dying day. I was worried that this searing pain would never go away. What did they know of my circumstances that they so openly spoke to each other about? None of them even knew what acid was before I was attacked with it.

I broke down. I pushed my head into my hands and let out a howl. Everyone stopped talking to look at me, in shock. 'Shut up. Shut up. All of you. The reason I am here is because of you. You all decided whom Gulshan should marry. You decided that she should go back to her husband after Saufi was born and you knew he was troubling her for money. You and this goddamn society is why I am in this situation. It's a curse to be a girl in this world because of people like you. How dare you sit here and talk about how sad it is that this has happened to me? How dare you sit here and tell me that it will be okay? No, it will not be okay, you hear me? I hate you all. Leave, please leave.'

Ammi gasped. 'I am so sorry. She's been like this for a while now. But, of course, it's only natural after what she's been through.' A visitor offered me some water, which I declined. She touched me on my arm and walked away. They clicked their tongues in sympathy and continued to talk about how my outburst was normal and expected. I wiped my tears and went back to sleep.

What was the point of carrying on? It's not like they ever heard me. Nothing changed. They continued to talk about me as if I wasn't there. Not only was I screaming for help, I was now invisible as well.

11

Depressed, But Not Mad

I WAS BREATHING. BUT now that I had seen my face I had become even more withdrawn. I wouldn't even eat unless I was forced to eat by Ammi. I stopped drinking water unless it was poured down my throat by Gulshan. I lay in bed all day and when I sat up, I simply stared at the wall. Words seemed distant and my depression became glaringly obvious to those around me.

Aizaz was worried about my future medical care. I knew he was, because in our one-room home, I could easily eavesdrop. One day I overheard my brothers talking about the multiple surgeries I would need, and they did not know how or where to arrange the money from. Abba had struggled enough and, my brothers, both of whom had jobs, wanted to help him financially. Riyaz was still a taxi driver, but Aizaz was working in a company. To contribute towards my medical costs, Aizaz took up a job that paid him five thousand rupees more than the last one. Borrowing money was no longer an option, because even our network of supporters came from limited means and Abba already owed friends and family lakhs of rupees.

My brothers asked a close relative for help during this uncertain time. She is a dearly loved relative and I have chosen to not reveal her identity due to the events that unfolded next. When she asked her husband to lend us money for my treatment, he became indignant and told her to cut off all ties with our family, calling us 'immoral'.

Such an injunction would seem irrational to a sound mind. This man, however, must have been conditioned to believe that insanity was rational. He refused to help us and unleashed his wrath on my relative, his wife. He believed that I must have done something wrong to instigate a 'good man like Jamaluddin' to attack me. 'Girls nowadays are really *chalu*. I don't know why Gulshan isn't supporting her husband. The whole family must have twisted minds. He obviously knew something about her that we don't.'

He was, in essence, implying that I was at fault. Perhaps I was having an affair with a man who could taint my family's image and Jamaluddin was simply trying to protect our family's honour?

I overheard the conversation and closed my eyes in disgust. I was so affected by this man's words that I stopped feeling hurt altogether. I became numb. Even my emotional barometer has its constraints.

I couldn't for the life of me comprehend why I had been attacked in the first place. I was just seventeen. I went to school, wore the hijab by choice, and had never even had a boyfriend. I had never spoken to Jamaluddin or his family except when conveying my regards at formal gatherings. I suppose I was attacked because I was the youngest daughter of the family and possibly the best target for revenge. A woman's worth in my country, and in so many places around the world, is often judged by her looks and her ability and willingness to be a dutiful wife and mother. By charring me alive, I think Jamaluddin believed he had insulted my entire family, especially his wife. By attacking me, I think Jamaluddin believed he had somehow tainted my social standing. That no matter where I went, people would shun me and my family, labelling me immoral, or why else would I have brought upon myself such an attack? Now I could never find a husband and settle down.

I had been home for around two weeks when I overheard people questioning my character and my role in bringing about the attack. They were trying to gauge just how terrible a thing I must have done to have been attacked so severely. In a way, they recognized the brutality of my attack. Yet, at the same time they insulted my situation by suggesting that no man would carry out such a vicious attack without cause. No man could be that crazy without a reason. I didn't know about 'victim-blaming' back then, but I believe that's what was going on.

It was after hearing these allegations that I decided to end my suffering once and for all. I no longer cared about anyone or how hurt they might be if I were gone. I felt sad at the thought of being shunned by society. The experience of the last two months had left me severely tortured and delusional. My family may mourn my loss in the short-term, but in the long run they would only benefit. I truly believed that I did not deserve to live and even if I did, I felt like I did not have the strength to carry on. What was there to look forward to?

I decided to take my life on 10 August 2014. I decided to plan my own murder, since in India, an attempt at taking your own life amounts to attempted murder. Suicide is basically illegal. I could be arrested for attempting to commit suicide.

Aizaz had informed me of the gruesome situation in Indian prisons after my first suicide attempt, and also that most suicide attempts were unsuccessful. Those who jumped from buildings were often left paralyzed, those who burnt themselves suffered through years of surgeries and grafts, those who took pills suffered severe liver damage and died slow, painful deaths from organ failures. I knew Aizaz told me these things because he wanted to drive away from my mind any further thoughts of suicide; he knew my weakness – fear of further physical pain. After my attack I feared pain more than death. Death was a gift I yearned for every single night.

Especially after I heard people's speculations about my attack I lost all faith in everyone and wished for instant death. What I was searching for was peace, and death was the only way I could attain it. I spent the whole day thinking about how to kill myself. The knives were locked up and I had no access to places I could jump from, no guns, no sleeping pills. The only option left was to hang myself. I was so desperate that even paralysis seemed a risk I was willing to take. So, on the morning of 10 August 2014, I planned out my suicide.

I hid a strong, sturdy dupatta under my pillow when no one was looking. I chose a strong cotton and polyester variety over the soft chiffon ones I owned. I didn't want it to tear mid-way and foil my death. I meditated over my suicide the whole day, yet no one seemed to pick up on the dangerous ideas spinning in my head.

After dinner, I closed my eyes and pretended to sleep for an hour or so. When I was sure everyone was fast asleep I quietly stood on the bed and reached for the ceiling fan. The lights were off and the room was dark. I made slow, deliberate movements because I was afraid of being discovered.

I raised my hands towards the fan and tried to throw the dupatta around it to create a noose. The bed creaked violently as I lost balance. I saw the lights flicker on before I could even regain my balance.

Aizaz had woken up from the disturbance. He switched on the flashlight on his phone and started shouting at me to stop when he saw me standing on the bed with a dupatta in my hands. By now everyone else had woken up. Aizaz quickly switched on all the lights. Ammi and Abba stared at me in shock, Gulshan rushed towards me and snatched the dupatta from my hands, and Riyaz began screaming. 'Is this how much you hate us?' he asked, pulling me off the bed. 'What will we do without you, Reshma? We're sorry, we are so, so sorry about everything. But please don't do this to yourself.'

Everyone had started crying. 'Imagine if Aizaz hadn't woken up,' said Ammi through her tears. 'Beta, if we had woken up to find you …'

'I want to die. Just let me die. Why are you punishing me by keeping me alive?' I cried, refusing to understand their pain.

'Reshma, life will get better,' Aizaz said. 'Trust me, it will. You can't give up now. If you do, we won't ever find happiness again. You are our world.'

For the next hour they sat by my side and consoled me. Abba spoke about all the dreams I had yet to accomplish – that I would go back to school, then on to university, and become a teacher one day. Aizaz tried to remind me of the things I loved. Samosas and biscuits, watching the seagulls fly around the ferries that docked right outside the Taj Mahal Palace Hotel, and my love for the movies. 'One day I'll make sure you meet your favourite actor. I promise.' I finally got tired of their charade and sought refuge in sleep. It was better to avoid conversations if they involved nothing but far-fetched promises.

But my family stayed up all night, even after I had fallen asleep. The lights were never switched off that night. Nor for the next one month. A unanimous decision was reached: Reshma was not to be left alone for a minute.

Someone or the other was watching over me twenty-four hours a day. At night, my family would take turns keeping an eye on me. Ammi would stay awake until midnight, Aizaz from midnight until 3 a.m., Riyaz until 6 a.m., Gulshan until noon. Come what may, I was not to be left unsupervised. They were going to make sure that there was no way I could take my life.

Apart from the suicide attempts, my constant state of misery also worried Aizaz deeply. He did some research and concluded that I was depressed, and suffering from post-traumatic stress disorder, which would need medical attention. He spoke to Abba and Ammi about taking me to a renowned mental health hospital in Kerala. My family agreed; they too were now worried that I may never communicate normally again. Since that fateful day I had stopped having conversations and the only words that reached their ears were those of anger, distrust, or my wish for death.

Chachu, Aizaz and I took a train to Kerala sometime in early September 2014. Aizaz had booked us at a small lodge. After breakfast, which I refused, we went straight to the hospital. As I walked in through the doors, fear swept over me. I was surrounded by people who seemed completely alien. They were crazy. I wasn't crazy! Men and women with no sense of their surroundings were roaming the hallways. Some were tugging at their own hair, others were crying for long-lost family members, while several more displayed strange repetitive behaviour, clapping their hands or pointing at every bird that flew by the window. I saw a woman screaming as she was held down by security officers and taken back to her room.

This was a veritable house of horrors. This was my first time in a *pagal khana*, a place for the truly insane, those quite beyond help. In this country, people with mental illnesses are still considered crazy, mad, psychotic. Their families are crippled by poverty and illiteracy, and thus the patients are left to rot at such hospitals. Many believe that these patients are possessed. As kids, our siblings would tell us we would be taken to the pagal khana if we misbehaved. It is a living version of hell and my brother had willingly brought me here.

I felt so scared. Dark thoughts raced through my mind. Perhaps if I tried to talk to my brother he would believe I was normal. 'What are we doing here?' I asked, casually trying to make conversation. I needed him to know I was still sane. Depressed, but not mad.

'We're here to see a really good doctor,' Aizaz replied. We waited outside the doctor's office for our appointment and I kept staring at the floor. I was too scared to look at the people around me. Screams echoed through the hallways.

We entered the doctor's office when our wait was finally over. He motioned for me to sit right next to him, and Aizaz and Chachu sat opposite him. 'So, tell me, beta – what happened?' he asked me. I didn't respond. My case file was lying right in front of him. Why couldn't he just open and read it? Aizaz began reciting my story. 'Would have been nice to hear it from her,' the doctor replied. I hated him. One more person pretending I wasn't there.

'What are her symptoms?' he asked Aizaz. Aizaz filled the doctor in about everything that wasn't mentioned in the file: my depression, my lack of appetite, the suicide attempts, my inability to participate in conversations. 'She just stares at the walls all day.'

Well, what would you expect me to do?

After listening to Aizaz for half an hour and not making a single attempt at speaking to me again, the doctor reached his well-informed decision. 'We must admit her here.'

I gasped in shock. 'No,' I said. 'I'm not mad. I don't belong here with these lunatics.'

I know my words were harsh and unfair to the inhabitants of the hospital, but my mental strength had been severely compromised by the trauma I had recently been through. My chachu looked at me and asked us to step outside. 'Let's talk about this, beta,' he said as Aizaz and I followed him out of the doctor's office.

'We can't possibly leave her here,' he said. 'It's so far away from home, Aizaz, and right now Reshma needs her family more than anything else. These places are dangerous. We don't know what they'll do to her here. You know that they use electric shock treatments on their patients, right? What if they electrocute Reshma?'

I began to cry. I begged my brother: 'Please, bhaiya. Please don't leave me here. I promise I will never try to kill myself again, but I'm not crazy. I'm just sad and depressed. I'm not crazy. Don't leave me here to die.'

Aizaz was torn between wanting to save my life and to grant me some comfort. Eventually, he was swayed to decide in my favour by Chachu's contributions to the conversation. Mental health services are still outdated in our country, and one often hears horror stories emerge from hospitals meant for mental health patients. Beatings, electrocution, rape, isolation are common punishments in such hospitals. I had already suffered enough and I was a young girl. Any further trauma could potentially break my spirit. After a lengthy discussion between Chachu and Aizaz, it was decided that I would not be admitted here.

We returned to the doctor's clinic and a consensus was reached. While the doctor still believed that I should be admitted to the psych ward, he could not force his decision against my will without Aizaz and Chachu's consent. Instead, he prescribed anti-depressants and told Aizaz to regularly follow up with a psychiatrist in Mumbai.

I was on these anti-depressants for a little over a month. It was an escape from my reality. I would sleep all day and night, waking up only for meals, showers, and doctor's appointments. Throughout September that year, Aizaz worked hard to find a solution to my depression. I still needed at least a dozen immediate surgeries, but before the dates for these could be fixed, he insisted on determining whether I was psychologically fit for further treatment.

Every week he would take me to a therapist, with whom I would never speak. I would just sit there in silence till the sessions ended on their own. On 16 September 2014, my therapist wrote a little note on the side of my chart, clearing me for further surgeries. It meant I was emotionally ready.

Patient had acid thrown on her four months ago, has sleep disturbances, low moods, anorexia, low concentration, fatigue, avoidant behaviour, occasional flashbacks. Advise: stick to anti-depressants. There are no contraindications for surgery from psychiatry point of view.

This doctor was my knight in shining armour. She was the first person I had met who saw my behaviour as normal. While my family and friends continued to try and 'normalize' me, they didn't realize my behaviour was already rather 'normal' for someone in my situation. They wanted me to be the same old Reshma, but the same old Reshma hadn't been through what I had. Trauma, violence, despair: they change people. I had become extremely conscious of myself around my family. In their presence, my shoulders would tense up and I would start worrying about where my hands were, my posture, where I was looking, how quickly or slowly I was eating, or if I was breathing right. I was afraid of being perceived as crazy and I never wanted to enter a psychiatric hospital again. I tried to speak as well, but by the time I would string together an appropriate sentence in my mind and muster the courage to say it out loud, the right moment would have passed.

This doctor was the first person to validate my emotions. I didn't mind sitting in silence with her because it was comforting. I could be who I was without fear of repercussions. I could slouch lower into the couch and say 'no' to the water she would offer, simply because I wasn't thirsty. If I said 'no' around my family they blamed it all on my depression and asked me to try to be happy again. On a couple of occasions, I told the doctor about the pain I was in, and she just nodded. Not once did she say that everything would be alright. For that, I am eternally grateful.

Now that I was cleared for surgeries, Aizaz had a monumental hurdle to cross. My nose needed reconstruction, my face and ears needed numerous skin grafts, my lip had fused with my chin and needed to be separated and reconstructed, and my right eyelid needed to be enlarged since the skin around it had fused and become circular, instead of the oval it had been earlier. Since it was the only eye I could see with, this surgery was of immediate urgency.

We had no money for further surgeries and borrowing was no longer an option. Aizaz reached out to every NGO he could, hoping someone would be able to foot the bills. In this process, he learnt of a man named Vivek Shukla, who connects those in need with those who offer help. So many of us in India struggle to find help because we don't know where to look and because of the lack of a proper network, NGOs struggle to find beneficiaries. On 1 October 2014, Aizaz wrote to Mr Shukla:

hi mr vivek,, this is aizaz reshma qureshi brother... acid attack on reshma on 19 may 2014.. attack is done in mauaima allahabad. i am sending you her photograph before acid attack photo or after the acid attack photo.. plz help us mr vivek.... we are in lot of problem right now.... we are in mumbai right now for her treatment.. plz help us.

regards, aizaz.

Attached with this email were my photographs and a scan of a Hindi news article recounting my story. The headline read: 'Kaash Usne Maut Di Hoti' ('I Wish He Had Granted Me Death'). Little did we know that this email would change the course of our lives.

12

Make Love Not Scars

WHILE I WAS DEALING with the gruesome aftermath of my attack, a young woman halfway across the world was busy studying fashion at the Leeds Arts University. Barely twenty-one, she had stumbled across a picture of an acid-attack survivor while browsing the internet in her bedroom.

She had vowed to find purpose in fashion while at university. But after struggling and failing to do so, she left, and returned to India sometime in the summer of 2014, camera in hand, hoping to shoot a documentary on acid-attack survivors. When she realized the true extent of the atrocities such survivors face in this country, she decided to launch a full-fledged organization instead to rehabilitate and empower these women. (The university eventually granted her an honorary degree for her work at Make Love Not Scars, the non-profit organization she founded in New Delhi.)

On 2 October 2014, Vivek Shukla forwarded Aizaz's email to this young woman. At this time, Ria Sharma was in the process of getting the paperwork in order so she could register her NGO. She had no idea what Make Love Not Scars would turn into eventually, and all she tried to do back then was help the cases that came her way in whatever capacity she could. We didn't know she had only worked on two or three cases at the most when Aizaz was put in touch with her. While I had just been attacked with acid, she had just realized exactly what life post acid attack entailed. We were like two lost deer, trying to not get blinded by headlights.

I needed surgeries and before anything else, that is what Ria focused on arranging for me. She called Aizaz on 3 October on his cell phone. None of us had a clue who Ria was, or how long she had been working in this field. She was ready to help us and that was all we needed to know.

The last acid-attack survivor she had helped had received treatment from a renowned surgeon I will call Dr Jain for the purposes of this book. Ria had fixed an appointment for me with Dr Jain on 8 October at his clinic. She told Aizaz not to worry about funds; all we had to do was turn up, and she would handle the rest. Dr Jain came highly recommended. His skills as a surgeon were supposed to be extraordinary and he had been awarded some of India's highest civilian awards.

The same day, to obtain funds for my surgeries, Ria wrote to individual donors and set up a crowdfunding campaign on Indiegogo, an international crowdfunding website based in San Francisco, California. The goal was to raise around 1 lakh rupees, or 2,200 US dollars. Aizaz helped Ria with whatever material she needed for the campaign. My pre-attack and post-attack photographs were published on the campaign page along with my story. Back then Indian non-profits relied heavily on raising funds through door-to-door calls for donations, placing donation boxes at stores, and simply making cold calls. However, the rise of crowdfunding platforms was slowly levelling the playing field for those new to the non-profit field with no networks and resources. There were very few non-profits that were crowdfunding at that time in India, and Ria regularly updated Aizaz about the campaign's progress. She made it clear that she had run less than a handful of crowdfunding campaigns prior to mine and that each one had been a struggle. None of us expected to collect too many donations online. While we were busy crowdfunding, a private donor from Ria's network donated some money directly to the hospital since I was expected to go in for a surgery anytime over the next few days, depending on Dr Jain's initial assessment and availability.

I had my first appointment with Dr Jain on 8 October 2014, just five days before I was to turn eighteen. I accompanied Ammi and Aizaz to the clinic with a heavy heart, fearing the toll the surgeries would take on my body. I wanted nothing more than to leave all my pain behind, and to intentionally assault my body with more cuts and stitches was a harrowing idea.

We walked in through the clinic doors and were shown to the waiting area. There were benches lined against the walls and we sat down, facing a row of people. I leaned back and closed my eyes. 'Kya hua, beta?' I heard Ammi ask someone.

'Aunty, acid attack,' a girl responded.

I opened my eyes to see who Ammi was talking to. Normally, I would have ignored the conversation and pretended to be asleep, but this was the first time I would be face to face with another acid-attack survivor. I suddenly realized how odd it was that in the five months since my attack I had never heard of another acid-attack survivor. At last, I was in close proximity to someone just like me. Without ever having spoken to her, I felt like we could be great friends someday.

My heart began to race; for the first time in months I felt excited. I opened my eyes to find bandages covering the girl's forehead and nose. Her nose must have been the size of my fist. I wondered what she looked like without those bandages. I shuddered at the thought.

What surprised me though was how rapidly she spoke. Here I was, almost never having said a word to strangers since my attack, and this young woman, sitting across from my mother, was hurling words like spitfire. She was laughing and cracking jokes, asking Ammi about me, and relating her unpleasant experiences to the nurses. Me, she never spoke to, though. Maybe she knew how I felt. I kept looking at her, not moving an inch of my body. If she had tried speaking to me, I wouldn't have known what to say.

Five minutes later a nurse came to fetch me. 'Reshma. And Laila (whose real name, too, shall be withheld). Dr Jain will see you now.' We were supposed to go in together? I got up and followed Laila into the doctor's office. She smiled as she held the door open for me. I looked over at her and smiled back. In that moment, she felt like a kindred spirit. This was the first stranger I had smiled at since my attack.

We stood quietly as the doctor fumbled through some paperwork. There were two empty chairs right in front of him, but he never offered them to us. When he was done he looked up. 'Ah, you're here,' he said to me. 'Take a look at Laila. I did most of her surgeries. Laila, remove your bandages.'

Without hesitation, Laila did as told. I looked away when she started unwrapping her face. It felt slightly odd for me to witness another's wounds. An uncomfortable thought kept playing in my mind: if I, an acid-attack survivor myself, was afraid of Laila's injuries, how afraid did regular strangers feel when they saw me? I looked at Laila from the corner of my eye and then looked away, an uneasy knot forming in my stomach.

'Come here,' Dr Jain motioned to me to move closer to his desk. I walked over and he showed me photographs. 'This was Laila before her attack, this is Laila after her attack. She had no nose, you see?' I felt anxious. He was talking rapidly and with force. He hadn't even asked me my name or said hello. He held my arm tightly as he pointed at Laila's injuries in the photographs. I didn't want to look because in those photos she looked wretched. 'She had forty-five surgeries under me.' I began to feel scared of this doctor.

If I thought my injuries were bad, I wondered how Laila had survived hers. Her nose had completely burnt off and that's why it was so big after reconstruction. In time it would shrink, but it would remain bulbous forever. Her entire face had to be grafted and she had lost both her ears. In fact, there was merely a hole where her right ear used to be. For months no patient would agree to take the beds next to hers because of how grotesque she looked. Her screams would haunt the ward for days and nights. Her mother was dead, and her father worked all day. She was alone, and even the nurses were afraid of seeing her up close when they had to administer her medicines. People were scared to even look at her. They still felt that way, he said.

I finally took a good look at Laila. She was just standing there smiling as the doctor pointed at various parts of her face and bragged of his success. 'She doesn't look that scary anymore, does she?' I was disgusted at how she was being put on display for me. 'Go, stand next to her,' Dr Jain said.

I was already afraid of this man, but I had no choice because I was dependent on him for my treatment. His success in plastic surgery spoke for itself, plus we wouldn't have to worry about the financial aspect with him. He then pointed out my injuries to Laila and she nodded, sighing. I believe she had got used to the drill. I hated every moment of that interaction.

It felt odd, the way the situation had panned out. The doctor had brazenly invaded our privacy. We were, at the end of the day, acid-attack survivors, yet strangers to one another. He had discussed the most personal details of our medical history and our emotional state without paying heed to the fact that perhaps having the right to narrate my own story to those I thought worthy was the only way I was able to maintain some dignity. I was stripped naked by hospital staff, considered crazy by many, pitied by most, and forgotten by some. At the very least, I felt I had a right to my own story. I didn't mind Laila knowing my story, but I would have liked to have told her myself. My story should be mine to tell.

'Your surgery will be on the 14th of October,' Dr Jain said to me when he was done highlighting to Laila my facial flaws. I looked at him in disgust. Laila had been brought in simply as an emblem of his success. Neither had he asked me a single question about my condition prior to announcing my surgery date, and I still had no idea what sort of surgery he would perform. I simply nodded and walked out, feeling deeply intimidated. Laila followed suit.

At the doorway, she stopped and smiled at me again. This time I decided to speak to her.

'Who did this to you?'

'A relative,' she said.

'Same,' I replied.

She nodded. 'It'll get better. I used to feel so depressed. I just wanted to die. Everywhere I went, people would stop and stare, or avert their eyes in fear. I felt as though I was no longer a human being. I've now decided that I should not have to suffer because of our society. I did nothing wrong, so why should I be the one to cower in fear? It'll get better, Reshma, trust me. There are many acid-attack survivors like you and me out there. Some of them have jobs and some are even married with children! I'll get married one day, trust me, and I'll wear a big red, poufy lehenga on my wedding night, too. You'll never look as good as you did before, but you will look and feel a lot better than you do right now! Don't let this ruin your life.'

I laughed and just like that my heart felt lighter. Laila's happiness was infectious and that day I went home with a newfound sense of hope. The minute Laila entered my life, I knew things would get better. Receiving encouragement and hope from another acid-attack survivor was extremely different from the opinions of those who had never suffered the same fate. If Laila, with her horrific injuries, could have found her voice again, I knew I would, too, one day. After five months, I suddenly found myself longing again. I longed to meet more acid-attack survivors. I knew that their stories would lead me towards my own inner strength.

I joined Ammi and Aizaz as I wished Laila goodbye with a smile on my face. Aizaz looked at Ammi incredulously. Laila and I exchanged numbers and I told Aizaz I was scheduled for surgery on 14 October, one day after my eighteenth birthday. Aizaz went to the nurse to get more information and soon we were on our way home. I was hungry and I asked to have biryani for dinner. Ammi laughed out loud and immediately sent Gulshan out to buy some meat. This was the first time since my attack that I had willingly asked for a meal.

13

Under the Knife

I WAS TO BE admitted to Bombay Hospital on 14 October. A private donor had already funded my upcoming surgical procedures and the funds raised through crowdfunding were to be utilized for further medical procedures. But due to an unprecedented turn of events, we had to bring the campaign to a close earlier than we had planned.

Within ten days of launching the campaign, we had reached an end goal that was 407 per cent higher than our target goal. My story had touched hearts across the globe and had, as they say, gone viral. Although surprised at how far my story had spread, we were also relieved to learn that Ria had successfully crowdfunded around 9,000 US dollars for my medical care. Money was no longer a cause of stress for my family and Abba could now focus on dedicating his savings towards paying back loans. More funds could be raised as and when required. Private donors were now writing to us from all corners of the world and we were forced to turn away donations so that they could be utilized elsewhere.

Ria called Aizaz, beyond excited at the outcome. 'This is working beyond my wildest dreams!' Aizaz handed me the phone and I told Ria how thankful I was. She did the talking for the remainder of the conversation and I was glad for that, because the more she spoke the more comfortable I started to feel with her. There was no need for forced conversation. She said that the money had been transferred directly to the hospital and that I was free to get any treatment I wished. A small sum, around ten per cent of the money raised, was sent to my family to cover miscellaneous expenses, such as our travel and food, while I was to be in surgery. The fact that she had thought of all the small matters touched my heart. Very few people understood the state of our poverty back then. Our hearts would bleed every time we had to pay an auto driver, so Ria's gesture meant the world to us.

I turned eighteen on 13 October 2014. Over the course of my journey, 13 October has come to be of great significance to a number of people in my life. As I entered adulthood, that date brought with it the promise of a new beginning. I had found an incredible support system, had guaranteed funding for my surgeries, and was now connected with other acid-attack survivors through Ria and Laila. I was slowly becoming happier and Ammi had already put away my anti-depressants a week ago. A few days after Ria and I met at the clinic, I discovered that she and I shared the same birthday. I turned eighteen, and she, twenty-one. Two years later, I would meet the woman with whom I was to write my memoir, Tania Singh, who came to Make Love Not Scars as a volunteer and became its CEO. When I told her I was turning twenty on 13 October 2016, she laughed. 'I was supposed to be born on the thirteenth, but I was far too impatient. My birthday is on 11 October. But guess what? It's my parents' anniversary on the thirteenth!' The three of us get along really well, being Librans and all that, and October has proven to be a lucky month every year ever since.

Back then, however, I didn't think much of the date. In 2014, 13 October was the day before I was to undergo another excruciating procedure. I had not eaten or had any water; I had to be on an empty stomach before they could administer general anaesthesia. We left for the hospital at around 5 a.m. and Ria called every hour since, checking in on us and making sure we were comfortable.

I remember feeling scared and lonely. I didn't even know what surgery I was going in for. Later that morning, Dr Jain arrived with his team. 'All ready?' he asked. I nodded. He was so intimidating that even if I hadn't been ready, I wouldn't have had the courage to say otherwise. I noticed how people walked on eggshells around him. The minute he entered my room, the nurses fell silent. His team walked behind him, moving out of the way as he paced up and down the room.

'Today, first off, we will fix the upper eyelid on your right eye. We will do a full thickness graft; the graft will come from your right arm. We will also fix your lips and mouth.' He went on to use big medical terms we could not understand. The progress report later stated that he had released the ectropion upper lid and performed full thickness graft on my right eye, taken from the medial side of my right arm. The ectropion upper lip, nasolabial region, and the columella were released ... and more procedures, the details of which I don't wish to bore you with.

I was, of course, petrified. I was receiving this treatment five months after being attacked with acid. The only surgery I previously went through was a skin graft on my forehead, and I still remember the immense pain I had woken up with. I remember how much I had cried every time I had to walk because the skin between my thighs, from where the graft had been harvested, had still not healed. I couldn't understand how they would operate on my eyelid. What if I went completely blind?

I nudged Aizaz so he would ask the doctor for more details. Aizaz asked the doctor if he could simplify his explanations for us. His response shocked me beyond belief. Even today, when I think of how harmful words can be, I think of Dr Jain.

'Please, I don't have time for all this nonsense. First you people get your daughters and sisters married to awful men and then cry over the outcome. When are you going to learn?' Leaving us with these insensitive words, he stormed out of the room, his team following on his heels. I noticed a young female doctor turn back to look at me. She gave me a gentle smile, as if apologizing for the doctor's behaviour.

A silent, uncomfortable lull filled the room. I could see how the doctor's words had affected my family and I started to feel angry. How could this stranger, who knew absolutely nothing about us, make such an audacious statement? Did he have even an ounce of an idea how hard my family had struggled to cope with our predicament? It's not as though any of us had known of Jamaluddin's violent streak. No parent purposely wished such a fate upon any of their children. My parents had big dreams for all their children. They believed that Gulshan would have a happy married life with a husband who would prove to be a doting father. Had they known of his cruelty, they would have never arranged for her to marry him.

With only a few words, Dr Jain had stereotyped an entire generation of abused women. The way he said 'you people' had dripped with so much contempt that we felt subhuman. It was clear that he thought himself superior to us. I felt offended at the pain he had caused my family. As it was I was suffering endlessly and now we had to deal with this thoughtless doctor, who had been a part of our lives for just a few hours, yet claimed to know everything about 'us people'. What did he know about the months when my family gave up on sleep or rest just to ensure that I wouldn't take my own life? Did he have a clue about the way Abba denied our family basic necessities so that I could sleep in an air-conditioned room. It was at this precise moment that I realized an educated man isn't necessarily the wisest.

'Forget what he said,' I mumbled, as I watched Abba wipe away a tear. 'I never meant those things I said, Abba.' It was time to apologize for all occasions on which I had held my family responsible for my attack. My PTSD had led me to harbour delusional beliefs. While that is no excuse for my bad behaviour, there was also no justification for the way the doctor had lashed out at us.

'Don't worry about it. We all know that the most important thing is to make sure Reshma gets better. Let's not bother him with unnecessary questions. He's a famous and important doctor. He probably got annoyed that we were taking up his time and said things in anger. He probably knows more about Reshma's medical needs than we do, anyway,' a dejected Aizaz said. I could tell he was trying to make Ammi and Abba feel better just like I was.

I pulled through the surgery and woke up in pain and had to stay at the hospital for four more days. The next round of surgeries was set for 21 October. Although that surprised me, I just wanted to be over with it all. After the next round of procedures, I was allowed some respite until the third round which was slated for December.

Sometime in the beginning of November, Aizaz received a call from Ria. 'I'm coming to Mumbai!' She was excited about meeting us at last. Although we had never met in person, her help had been monumental. We were also dying to meet her.

We would meet Ria on 11 November. That morning I had no idea what to expect. 'Ria ma'am must be so kind,' said Ammi. We walked into Dr Jain's clinic for my post-operative follow-up. I was nervous. Ammi and I sat in the waiting room, where we were to meet Ria. Ten minutes later a young girl walked right up to me and hugged me without warning. 'Hi Reshma, how are you? Do you recognize my voice? It's me, Ria!' I couldn't believe it was her. *Impossible*, I thought to myself. She's so young ... and beautiful. I couldn't help but wonder what her journey had been like for her to end up here with me in a hospital waiting room.

I looked at her in awe and noticed Ammi was doing the same. I wasn't really sure, but I had imagined Ria Sharma to be a woman in her thirties or forties. But this girl in front of me looked as though she was my age!

I nodded hello and sat down against the wall, observing her make conversation with Ammi. Her cheerfulness, like Laila's, was infectious. Not once did she look at me and sigh or treat me like a broken doll. She treated me like she would treat any other seventeen-year-old. I felt an instant connection with her and later discovered she too had felt the same way. We were important to each other in ways I can't explain. She told me that when she had found out I was just seventeen, her heart had rooted for my recovery. 'You're younger than me, and far more powerful.' I told her the same. I was fascinated that a young woman who had just turned twenty-one could change lives in such an incredible manner, and that too in India where no one took women seriously.

Ammi thanked Ria profusely and then broke down. '*Arre*, why are you crying, aunty? Everything is okay. Look! Reshma's right eye is totally fine now and she's getting better fast. Don't worry, soon we'll get her started with English and computer classes. She will find a job and have an amazing life.'

We were called into the doctor's office. Ammi decided to wait outside. I was her weakness, and she could no longer bear to watch me suffer more pain. 'Come, let's go.' Ria held my hand and led me to the office. 'Are you feeling shy?' she asked. I nodded. She laughed. 'Don't worry, I get shy too. By the way, what do you think of the doctor? I don't know much about him, but I've heard he's amazing!'

I didn't say anything because I had nothing pleasant to say about Dr Jain. We walked into his office and Dr Jain greeted Ria. 'Come here, Reshma,' he said, indicating that I should stand next to him. Ria helped herself to a chair. He hadn't offered her a seat, but she didn't seem to care. I liked that.

He pulled out his laptop and positioned it such that Ria and I could both see the screen. 'I'm going to show you a video of one of Reshma's surgeries.'

'What? No, Dr Jain, please,' said Ria. 'That would be unnecessary.'

'No, it's important,' he said with a tone of finality. He made me stand there, like he had done with Laila, and pointed at my surgical scars, my eyes, nose, and the grafts, as the video kept rolling. I began to cry and cried throughout his presentation. Not once did he try to comfort me. Ria told me to stop watching, a suggestion which the doctor ignored. I felt sick to my stomach as he made me watch the entire video, telling me how he wanted me to know exactly what he had done. The way he had cut my face, the pieces of skin he used as grafts, the red, bloody, raw skin he had tried to heal – he made sure that every detail of his success was etched in our minds. Ria tried to put a stop to this circus in vain.

We left the office, feeling deeply unsettled. 'He's scary,' said Ria as we walked out. I nodded. She sighed. 'Forget it, you're going to get better soon and you will never have to enter this clinic again.'

14

#EndAcidSale

I AM NOT SOMEONE who allows anger to cloud my judgement. While Dr Jain did lack basic decency and empathy towards his patients, his techniques and medical knowledge were, without a doubt, extraordinary. The next time I went under the knife was on 21 October 2014, and then on 23 December 2014, and again on 21 April 2015.

My previous graft had taken one hundred per cent to my eye, which was a good sign. The alternate stitches were now removed and any extra tissue was trimmed, thereby significantly improving the vision in my right eye. I could now read and write fine print, which I found difficult earlier. I underwent some other procedures for my eyes, mouth, scalp, and some facial reconstruction as well.

I was still struggling with depression, but I finally had someone who understood depression better than most people I knew. Ria had decided that I needed someone to talk to, though not necessarily her. 'No matter what, I never wanted you to feel obligated to talk to me.' She believed she had entered my life as a person who helped me get medical care, and did not wish to be the one calling me every day because she feared I might feel compelled to speak to her out of obligation. A therapist wasn't ideal either, for similar reasons. It had to be more unconditional, someone who could be my friend.

Back then, Ria did not have a team and was managing Make Love Not Scars alone. She would often call in favours from her family and friends. One of her friends from school, Mehr Sandhu, offered to speak to me. She was also twenty-one at the time. Every day, for months, she would call me at 5 p.m. on the dot and speak to me for forty-five minutes to an hour. I would only say hello and she would talk even when I was unresponsive. It was often the happiest hour of my day. I think Mehr and Ria's strategy was to edge me back into normal life by showing me a glimpse of what regular lives were like. We were, after all, very close in age and shared similar interests. I think, like Ria, Mehr was also bothered by how young I was. Mehr would talk about make-up, her favourite lipsticks, the drama that went down at her university, and I would automatically be engrossed. I asked her what university life was like and she told me in entertaining detail. 'Don't worry, you'll go one day.' And that's how I began dreaming of going to university.

I started looking forward to these phone calls. Aizaz bought me a smartphone so I could download WhatsApp and get more out of my friendship with Mehr.

I believe change is so gradual that one never notices it when it creeps into one's own life. I never noticed how I was changing, but everyone around me could see it. I was slowly becoming more confident and sometimes took the initiative to call Ria and Mehr to share what had happened in my day, if anything had happened at all. Ria would often talk about wanting nothing more than to make a difference for women in India and I would agree profusely. 'In what other country is a seventeen-year-old treated like an object of revenge?' I would say. 'In another country, my biggest worry would be passing my exams and not being attacked with acid, raped, or killed. When I get better, I would like the whole world to know my story.'

'Trust me, the world will know your story,' Ria said. 'As long as you're willing to do the talking, I'll handle the rest.' Back then I thought it was nice to dream of such things, but little did I know that Ria had made a promise to herself that day. She kept her eye out for opportunities and directed them towards me.

Ria convinced me to start giving small interviews here and there for the print media as well as some local television channels. I agreed because I now wanted to channel my anger towards making a positive change. After meeting Ria and other acid-attack survivors, I was beginning to discover the numerous possibilities at my behest. I said yes to every opportunity that allowed my voice to be heard. Plus, it was always something to look forward to. Every time I saw my name in the papers, or watched a clip of a television interview, I was filled with a sense of pride, and more than that, a sense of purpose. I had nothing else in my life. No education, no career, no husband or children, and barely a face. All I had was my voice and my newfound convictions.

One day, towards the end of May 2015, I received a phone call from Ria. 'Reshma, you won't believe what's happened. There's this huge advertising agency, Ogilvy & Mather, and they want to do a pro bono campaign for Make Love Not Scars this year! Remember how you said that you want the whole world to know about acid attacks? I think this is our chance.'

Just that year, two creative heads at Ogilvy & Mather in Mumbai – Harshik Suraiya and Geetanjali Jaiswal – had stumbled upon some coverage surrounding acid-attack survivors. They were deeply moved by the images they saw and decided to reach out to organizations that helped such survivors in India. They came up with the idea to run a campaign to raise awareness about the rampant epidemic of acid attacks across the country. In the beginning of 2015, Make Love Not Scars had just been registered, had no funding, no help, and minimum social media or even traditional media presence. No one had heard of us. Obviously, we weren't Harshik and Geetanjali's first choice. We were, in fact, the last. When they reached out to the larger non-profits, they were disappointed to find that the management of those organizations did not share their vision and believed their campaign would be futile.

At last, they came across a crowdfunding campaign that was hosted by Make Love Not Scars. With all other doors shut, Harshik and Geetanjali had no choice but to send an email to Ria. Pat came Ria's optimistic response. Harshik and Geetanjali's email said that Ogilvy & Mather was already working on a pro bono campaign around acid attacks. They hoped to meet some of the demands of acid-attack victims by running a campaign to implement the ban on the unregulated sale of acid in our country. They had lots of ideas, filmmakers on board, and were simply looking for an NGO partner with whom they could take things forward. Ria immediately picked up the phone and called Harshik.

The concept for the campaign was simple. Beauty tutorials were trending and no idea spreads as quickly as it does through viral content, we could all agree. A series of beauty tutorials conducted by an acid-attack survivor could provide audiences with the hard, cold facts about such attacks in India. These audiences, in return, would then be asked to sign a petition addressed to the Government of India.

In 2013, BBC reported that India sees approximately a thousand acid attacks a year. Based on ground research, Ria and Tania believe that the numbers are much larger. After all, Sweden, a nation of impeccable women's rights, reports a larger percentage of crimes against women than even my country. The rate of reported crime is more often a reflection of factors such as the victim's will to report it, various crippling socio-economic conditions, and the police's will to register that report, rather than an actual reflection of the crime rate itself.

Between 2012 and 2014, India had witnessed a staggering 250 per cent increase in the reported number of acid attacks. We wondered how many went unreported. Prior to 2013, India did not have designated laws around acid attacks. Then, on 19 July 2013, the Supreme Court of India directed all states and union territories to regulate the open sale of acid. It was shocking to witness such a rise in acid attacks despite the regulation. The petition drafted by Make Love Not Scars would request an implementation of the ban on over-the-counter sale of acid and a stronger implementation of the Poisons Act and Poisons Rules.

By 3 June 2015, Ria had convinced Harshik and Geetanjali that I should be the face of their campaign. Ria asked if I would be interested in shooting beauty tutorials that could potentially change the way the world viewed acid attacks. When one hears ideas that brave and meaningful, it's hard to say no, and I agreed without a second thought. I told my family that I was going to be the face of a campaign run in part by Make Love Not Scars. No one knew if it would have a significant impact, but we sure were overjoyed. Times were changing, I was changing, and Make Love Not Scars was evolving into something really admirable.

The process of shooting the campaign was long-winded, the final result miles ahead of the initial idea. The Ogilvy & Mather team spent a long time holed up in meetings with producers throughout the month of June. It was somewhat of a passion project for the team and they devoted their time and energies generously even as resources ran low. Somehow, we had to make it work.

The first working title of the campaign was #BeautyIsBrave. Notes were exchanged and ideas discussed in great detail. The official hashtag was to be

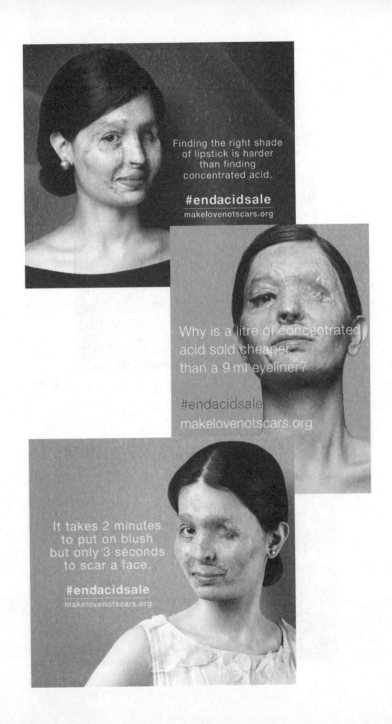

At a family wedding, a few months before I was attacked

In a hijab

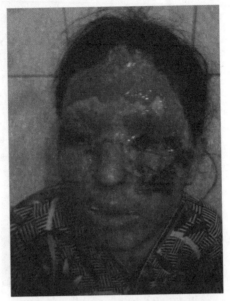

A few weeks after I was attacked

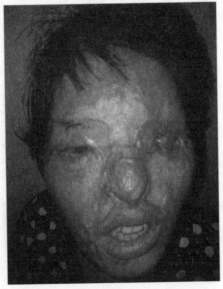

A few months after I was attacked

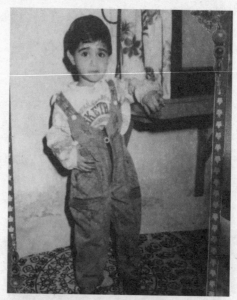

Throwback to my childhood days

*A budding friendship with Ria Sharma, founder of
Make Love Not Scars*

It's awards season for Beauty Tips by Reshma!

Make Love Not Scars wins the CNBC TV-18 Indian Business Leader Award for Brand of the Year

With a few survivors from Make Love Not Scars

Tania and me on the roof of our office

Ria and me at New York Fashion Week

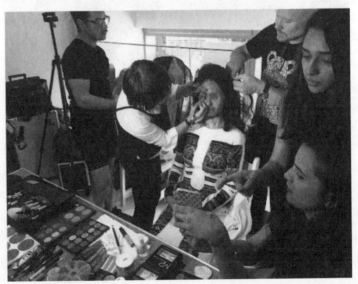

Hair and make-up for New York Fashion Week

Rehearsing for my first international ramp walk in New York

At New York Fashion Week

Walking the runway at New York Fashion Week

Sunny Leone and me

Shooting my documentary in New York

Just another take for my documentary

Shooting at Central Park, New York

From a day in my life

On the cover of Newsweek Middle East

With the King of Bollywood, Shah Rukh Khan

On my way to Los Angeles for some surgeries

With my brother Aizaz and his bride

My friend Soni and me with Jeremy Piven

With Dr and Deborah Alessi who are funding Soni's and my medical care in Los Angeles through the Face Forward Foundation

Soni and me with Caitlyn Jenner and her girlfriend at the Face Forward Gala in Beverly Hills

Winning the Kyoorius Creative Award for the #endacidsale campaign

The survivors and me at the Make Love Not Scars rehabilitation centre in New Delhi

#Thebeautytip. Since the idea was to make our petition go viral, it was decided that I would star in three to five videos that would be launched over a week. The more content we put out there, the more people come across it, which we hoped would directly translate into more signatures for our petition, which was to be linked to each video. But no matter how much progress we made with the scripts, something didn't feel right. We hadn't quite arrived at The Name.

And then it hit us. While beauty is brave, our goal was to end the open sale of acid. We decided to focus on our vision rather than our ideals, and the campaign was thus titled #endacidsale, an exact representation of what we were trying to accomplish through our petition. The official hashtag would be #BeautyTipsByReshma. By mid-June, Ria and the team at Make Love Not Scars were busy preparing the perfect petition for the Government of India – one which would later be linked to every video produced for the #endacidsale campaign.

Things were falling into place. The production house agreed to design the set at minimum cost, the directors were giving their time for free, we had found a location, the campaign had a great name, the petition was being diligently read and re-read, and finally, by 23 July 2015, all three scripts for the beauty videos were ready. We released the following three videos: Beauty Tips by Reshma: How to Get Perfect Red Lips; Beauty

Tips by Reshma: How to Apply Eyeliner; Beauty Tips by Reshma: How to Get Rid of Dark Spots Naturally

When I first read the scripts, I felt weak in my knees, and tears sprang to my eyes. Sometimes we come across a situation that seems so unfair that we can't help but cry, clench our fists and grit our teeth. Very rarely can we coherently translate this perceived injustice into words. The script for all three videos were so gut-wrenching because of how perfectly they translated the injustice of acid attacks into impactful words.

Each video was around a minute long, and the final message was that of a terrifying reality, and it became impossible to ignore the campaign's call to action. These videos can be found online, but I cannot help but include the transcript for one of them: How to Get Perfect Red Lips.

Hi girls! I'm Reshma. I'm here to teach you how to get perfect red lips. Start by brushing your lips; this removes dead skin and makes your lips rosy. Next, apply lip balm so that the lipstick doesn't dry. Use a lip liner; it should be the same colour as your lipstick. Now, apply the lipstick, only on the lips, not on the edges. Looks perfect, right?

Finally, the most important tip.

You will find a red lipstick easily in the market, just like concentrated acid. This is how, every day, a girl becomes a victim of an acid attack.

So, click on this link and help enforce the ban on the open sale of acid.

Effective, isn't it? With a script so simple yet powerful, I knew we would have thousands of people signing our petition. I believed in the #endacidsale campaign with every inch of my soul.

Since the campaign had to be produced on a strict budget, everyone needed to put in their best efforts and then some. No one had heard of Make Love Not Scars, and the Ogilvy & Mather team was just a small group of people with varying interests, but all deeply disturbed by the recent rise in acid attacks in the country. It was sort of like a pet project, one that we thought would either fail miserably, or create a little ripple on social media at best. The Make Love Not Scars Facebook page had less than 5,000 followers at that time, and our media presence was limited. There were also no donors with deep pockets to fund the #endacidsale campaign.

Despite these hurdles, Harshik and Geetanjali were working hard to finalize production, and Ria was in charge of hair, make-up and wardrobe. People were putting their own money into the campaign. Since I had never starred in a tutorial video or any video for that matter, everyone was sceptical that my lack of training might act as a hindrance. Ria asked the actress Amyra

Dastur to be present on the day of the shoot to make me feel comfortable in front of the camera. And she agreed!

We decided to shoot the campaign sometime in the beginning of July. Ria called Aizaz the previous night to give him the details of the venue and then spoke to me. 'Tomorrow will be a long day, a very long day. Rest well and don't be nervous. We're all here for you.'

I spoke to her for a while and could tell that she herself was anxious. She was excited, and very passionate about running this campaign, like a true activist. I felt a deep sense of respect for her. Before meeting Ria, my family was living under the weight of fear, anger and financial burdens, and within a few months since, I had had multiple rounds of free surgeries, made real friends, connected with other survivors, and, now, even had a significant purpose in life, to end the open sale of acid.

I woke up around 6 a.m. on the day of the shoot. As I got dressed, Ammi forced me to gulp down some tea and toast. It took me back to the day of my attack, for two reasons. First, Ammi had forced me to have the same breakfast before my Alimah exam, and, second, the day of the attack had been the last day I had left home with the purpose of gaining an education. Today was the first day I would leave home to impart an education. The wheels were turning and within a few months my role in life would change altogether.

Aizaz and I flagged down an auto and left for the local train station. The Mumbai locals are always crammed with thousands of people. People hang out of the train doorways, clinging to the poles on the sides of the doors as they make their way to their destination. I wedged my way into the women's compartment of the train, which is usually less crowded, and Aizaz stepped into the general compartment. We disembarked at Goregaon and took an auto to our final destination. Aizaz kept calling Ria because we couldn't find the address. 'Look up, just look up,' she said and we saw her standing on a balcony of an old building. Most of Mumbai has been torn down and rebuilt into apartments, but there were still some hidden treasures from generations ago, yet untouched by modern hands. This was one such structure. It exuded heritage.

A member of the Ogilvy & Mather team had found the perfect studio for the shoot location. Aizaz and I went inside and I looked around in wonder. People were barking instructions at each other. Upstairs, in a room with no windows, volunteers were setting up the background set. A baby pink background wall made of cardboard. Accessories were added: beautiful photo frames in pinks and blues, a bookshelf, some lamps, plants, and strings of fairy lights. 'With a topic this hard-hitting, we need to reel the viewers in with a welcoming warmth. We need to let them know that they have nothing to fear and that they'll be able to move on with their day without being damaged by what they see,' said one of the crew.

I understood their thought process. Often, when one talks about social causes, the atmosphere is dark and heavy, but the vision for #endacidsale was different. We wanted people, young and old, to receive our message without being intimidated by the messenger.

By then I had realized one thing, which was also weighing on the minds of everyone in the team. People often looked away when they saw me on the streets because my face was too gruesome for them. Something in people's soul shuddered at the sight of acid-attack survivors and on many occasions, social media sites such as Facebook, have removed photographs and videos of survivors because someone would flag certain content as 'graphic' and report it. This could pose a serious threat to our campaign. What if people skipped our message the minute they saw me? What if our reach was diminished? As a result, concessions had to be made. No video would last longer than a minute, light, airy music would play in the background, the set design would be friendly and warm, the shades would be all pastels, and I would be smiling throughout.

One might expect that images of acid-attack survivors should never be considered to be in violation of social media community guidelines, but this world is an odd place. Often, posts related to survivors have been flagged as violating community guidelines for being too graphic. I wish to ask the detractors why they feel they can object to the way we look. I am sure they have sensitive hearts. If they didn't, they wouldn't feel as anguished as they did.

While their emotional distress is an honourable reaction, I ask how they can turn their faces away or demand for our content to be removed because apparently it is too haunting for the viewers. It's not a choice for us. We can't change our faces or our stories, and we wish we weren't so painful to look at. Our faces are our reality, and nothing angers me more than when people say it is too much of an emotional burden to look at us. I say such people are weak and perpetrators of a system that compels us to cover our scars, implying that we should live with the injustice of our situation, while our attackers go scot-free.

I was handed three scripts to learn. I had been memorizing them at home as well, but I needed to practise diction, tone, articulation, pauses, dynamics, pace, and a gazillion other techniques for delivering my lines in the most impactful manner. Amyra and Ria sat with me for hours, making me go through the lines over and over again. I was practising my lines even after my hair and make-up was done, reciting them in my head as I changed into jeans and a T-shirt for the shoot, and refused to have tea because it would distract me. It was odd how much I was labouring over these words, when I had hardly spoken in the last few months. This time, though, what I had to say was the most important message I would deliver in my life so far.

We were ready to shoot by noon. We had just one day, and every minute counted. We didn't have the funds to rent equipment or request directors and sound producers to volunteer again. Doors and windows were closed to shut out all external noise and the entire team was asked to be as quiet as possible, so stray noise bites wouldn't creep into the sound recordings.

I sat on a chair and Ria quickly ran me through what accessories to pick up at what point during the shoot. I stumbled, making error after error. We tried again, I stumbled again. It wasn't working. I was unable to deliver the lines with impact while also manoeuvring lipsticks and eyeliners. A quick meeting was called and a change in strategy planned. I would do the actions and record a voiceover later.

We filmed for over twelve hours. We took a fifteen-minute lunch break, a fifteen-minute tea break, and occasional ten-minute panic-attack breaks during which Ria, Amyra and I would escape from the stern gazes of the Ogilvy & Mather team and unwind in a corner. At some point, perhaps some six or seven hours of shooting later, I looked at Ria and almost began to cry. 'I can't do it anymore. I just can't. Your expectations are way too high and the small details you're picking up on don't even matter. The words are powerful enough!'

The Ogilvy & Mather team wanted perfection and it was taking a toll on the Make Love Not Scars team because we had never shot videos before and did not understand how it was taking three to four hours to shoot a single one-minute video. That too without voiceover recordings. Eventually, at around 9 p.m., Ria put her foot down. Our work would never be perfect enough because of how important this was to each and every one of us, she said. We had to wind up by midnight, irrespective of where we stood. Strategies were changed again; I would deliver a sentence per take, which would later be edited into one final film. Finally around 2 a.m. we had the video footage we wanted. We decided to reconvene sometime later in the month to record the voiceovers in a recording studio. It was a long, difficult day and we saw tempers running high, patience wearing thin, but I do not regret a minute of it. At the end of the day we all hugged and cheered, knowing that despite our differences, we were in this together. Everyone snapped at everyone, yet no one held back an opinion because there was no fear of repercussion. We all wanted the same thing, to end acid sale, and what we had to do to get there was irrelevant.

I had never in my life witnessed such incredible energy, passion, professionalism and synergy in a team.

We met later that week itself to record the voiceovers. The video and audio had been collected, and from mid-July to mid-August, the Ogilvy & Mather team worked on editing the final Beauty Tips by Reshma videos for the #endacidsale campaign, while Ria and the Make Love Not Scars team of volunteers worked endlessly on fine-tuning the petition to the Supreme Court of India, ensuring a watertight stand against counter-arguments.

At around the same time, we were faced with a new challenge. Make Love Not Scars did not have an operational website. In the event that the campaign went well, we would need an informative platform for people to learn more about the organization. Aditya Bhandari owned a website design company called Hyper and offered his services for free. Throughout July, there were constant changes taking place with the video editing, the petition, and the website. This was an exciting month for Make Love Not Scars for several reasons. First, we were virtually unknown and this was going to be our big launch; second, we were creating a campaign at zero cost; and, third, people from all across the world were chipping in to help for free. It was exhilarating.

At last, the launch date of the campaign had been set: 31 August 2015.

15

A Storm of Change

THE THREE 'BEAUTY TIPS by Reshma' videos for the #endacidsale campaign were to be launched on three separate dates. Each video was linked to the petition. 'How to Get Perfect Red Lips' was to be launched on 31 August, 'How to Apply Eyeliner' on 2 September, and the third and final video, 'How to Get Rid of Dark Spots Naturally', on 4 September 2015. Since we had no advertising budget, we were hoping that by the time the second or third video was launched, some media interest would be generated and we would be able to crowdsource a respectable number of signatures for the petition.

Bharat Nayak, a member of the Make Love Not Scars team, also happened to be a core team member of a popular social media news platform called The

Logical Indian, or TLI, which continues to enjoy a loyal follower base. Ria convinced Bharat to bring TLI on board as the official media partner for #endacidsale and TLI agreed to share our campaign on their social media pages and their website. The first video, 'How to Get Perfect Red Lips' was uploaded to the Make Love Not Scars YouTube channel at 9 p.m. on 31 August 2015. A parallel article with an embedded video link was published on our Make Love Not Scars page and TLI's page on Facebook.

We kept our fingers crossed as our hearts beat loudly, but we kept a positive outlook throughout as the team celebrated the launch of what Ria and Tania lovingly call a zero-cost campaign with a million-dollar heart. Ria repeatedly said that with TLI on board we might be able to generate a few thousand views and signatures. With 25,000 signatures we would be able to influence the government to enforce the laws set by the Supreme Court that demanded the regulation of over-the-counter sale of acid. With the campaign up and running, there was nothing to do but hope for the best. By midnight, all our excited chatter had died down and the fatigue from having worked tirelessly over the past few days caught up with us. We went to bed tired but exhilarated.

No one had any grand expectations from the campaign. All we wanted was to reach out to a significant number of people and perhaps leave them with another cause to champion for. We were virtually unknown on the night we launched the #endacidsale campaign. The morning after, however, it seemed we had unknowingly taken the world by storm.

As we closed our eyes that night, #endacidsale began trending on Twitter and Facebook. Over 100,000 people signed our petition. Over 1 million people viewed the video on YouTube alone. Indians, Americans, Russians, Europeans, Australians, almost the entire world, really, was sharing our video and petition far and wide.

Ria woke up on 1 September 2015 to over a hundred missed calls on her phone, mostly from journalists, Harshik, and Bharat. Everyone's inboxes were flooding with every passing minute. Our website had crashed in the early hours of the morning. It was not built to handle any more than 10,000 visitors. During the five days of the social media campaign, our website crashed a total of six times. On that particular morning, the Ogilvy & Mather team had been desperately trying to contact Ria and Aditya, both of whom were sleeping soundly, not expecting to wake up to the storm of change we had created overnight.

Ria called me up right after she spoke to the folks at Ogilvy & Mather and had assured them that Aditya was out of bed and working on bringing the website back to life. Her voice was throbbing with excitement, and I swear I could hear her heart racing at the same pace as her rapid-fire words. 'Reshma, you've done it. Your voice is echoing in every corner of the world,' she kept saying. I felt my spirit soar higher than ever before. In that moment I knew I had found my life's true calling.

'Are you happy?' asked Ria.

'I will be once the government listens to us,' I told her.

'Let's make them,' said Ria. 'My phone is blowing up. I'm going to call back all the journalists, but you keep your phone by your side too, because I know they all want your number.'

And they did. The whole day Ria and I answered questions on our phone about what Make Love Not Scars stood for, why I had chosen to be the face of #endacidsale, and what we hoped to achieve through the campaign. Everyone at home watched me with an uplifting sense of pride. They had never witnessed this ferocity in me before, this unmistakable power in my voice as I spoke to the journalists. I don't speak much English, so Ria and Bharat handled the international media as I answered the questions the Indian media had for us. Everyone at home stayed as quiet as they could so as not to disturb me. At midnight, finally, I stopped taking calls. Ammi had made biryani and she stayed by my side until I finished eating, wiping tears of happiness and pride as I tried to get a grip on my excitement so I could eat a small bite before sleeping.

That day, 1 September 2015, was one of the happiest days of my life. For the first time, I felt proud to be a survivor. I had made several suicide attempts and suffered unimaginable pain, but I had finally overcome my trauma and become a part of something much larger than myself. The outcome of this campaign would result in saving and empowering thousands of women who fall prey to the abuse of over-the-counter sale of acid.

Over the next four days, the two other videos were released. At this point, we decided to launch a second phase of the campaign. Immediately, graphics were printed for billboards across Mumbai, with funding received from anonymous donors. These billboards had my face on it and featured messages that were at the heart of our campaign. 'It takes two minutes to put on blush but only three seconds to burn a face,' said one of them. 'Finding the right shade of lipstick is harder than finding concentrated acid,' said another. 'Why is a litre of concentrated acid sold cheaper than a 9 ml eyeliner?' was splashed on a third billboard. The messages haunted the city for weeks. I went to every billboard and took photos of myself standing below them. I felt proud and humbled.

By the end of September 2015, the entire world was listening to us. #Endacidsale triggered global conversations. The campaign, Make Love Not Scars, and my story, were covered extensively by the most influential newsmakers in the world. The *New York Times* ran the headline 'Indian Acid-attack Victim Makes a Bold Statement'; *Time* magazine said, 'This Beauty Tutorial Has a Surprisingly Powerful Message,'; and the *Wall Street Journal* called 'How to Get Perfect Red Lips' a 'Beguiling Beauty Video'.

Inside Edition ran a full feature on the campaign, screening my videos to the entire American population, while Marco Werman, critically acclaimed journalist and host of Public Radio International's *The World*, flew all the way to India to visit me at my home to shoot an interview and learn more about our mission. Politicians such as Sambit Patra, influencers like Jacqueline Novogratz and Sheryl Sandberg, and celebrities such as Sachin Tendulkar, Ashton Kutcher, Amy Poehler, and Amitabh Bachchan, spread the word further. We were featured in *People*, *Mirror*, *Cosmopolitan*, *RYOT*, Discovery Channel, the *Independent*, *Marie Claire*, *Huffington Post*, BBC, the *Daily Mail*, *Mashable*, and every leading Indian newspaper and magazine, among others.

By the end of September 2015, our petition had garnered over 350,000 signatures and our videos had been viewed millions of times. Ogilvy & Mather estimated that had the campaign been paid for, we would have had to spend over seventeen million dollars in public relations expenses. This is when #endacidsale began to be known as the zero-cost campaign with a million-dollar heart – the day we realized we had generated PR worth seventeen million dollars at zero cost!

The #endacidsale campaign began on 31 August 2015 and, on 23 May 2016, Indian states started enforcing the ban. Ria and I were ecstatic. Make Love Not Scars hadn't even completed a year when the campaign was launched. Ria was just twenty-two and I was nineteen. At that age, no one expects to witness such an incredible level of interest in their cause. But thanks to Ogilvy & Mather, TLI, our group of immensely dedicated volunteers, and our deep-vested interest in the cause, we had succeeded in achieving the impossible. From being virtually unknown, Make Love Not Scars had overnight turned into a force to be reckoned with, an organization to look up to for anyone working with or concerned about acid-attack survivors.

As a result of the campaign, Ogilvy & Mather India won numerous awards and accolades, including two Golds at the Effie India Awards 2015, one for direct marketing and the other in the Effie for Good category; the trophy for the latter sits proudly on Ria's desk at the Make Love Not Scars office. However, the proudest victory (apart from having states enforce the acid-sale ban) came when the campaign won a Glass Lion for Change and The Gold Lion for Film at the Cannes

Lions International Festival of Creativity 2016 in France. Ogilvy & Mather India became the first Indian agency to win the coveted Gold Lion in seven years; #endacidsale had brought it home!

September 2015 changed my destiny forever and propelled the rise of the non-profit that saved my life as it does today for so many who still suffer like I did. Needless to say, Ria and I became closer than ever before. We had triumphed against the odds – together.

16

Back to the Clinic

I MADE MY MARK as an anti-acid-sale activist after our humble launch and the insane success of the #endacidsale campaign. I agreed to every interview, showed up for every photo shoot, and spoke to every activist, government official, and non-profit partner Make Love Not Scars worked with. I repeated my story multiple times, until I could recite it in my sleep.

While I embraced my new sense of purpose, I was also made to feel as though what I was doing was futile. My distant relatives, neighbours, and detractors from various other quarters, would ask why I was giving so many interviews. Conspiracy theorists reared their heads with many unwarranted opinions.

I realized that many television journalists just want more ratings. The minute you are a sensation, the interview requests come flooding in, and soon money comes pouring into their exchequers. I stopped giving interviews unless I was paid.

Opinions came from all sorts of people, none of whom had ever been attacked with acid. I ignored them and carried on. I always believe that the first step towards change is awareness. If people aren't even aware of how easily acid is available, why would they ever campaign against its sale? I hadn't realized this before. I didn't care about being paid for my story or my time, neither was I interested in making a change overnight. I just wanted people to be aware; revolutions and protests only gain strength in numbers.

Meanwhile, my medical treatment came to an unexpected halt. Besides launching the #endacidsale campaign, I had also gone through multiple medical procedures that year. Sometime around December 2015, Dr Jain said that I would not be going under the knife for at least another six months. He called Ria and explained that general anaesthesia can be dangerous, especially after I had been through surgery as many times as I had. I needed more surgeries in the future, and so, needed to let my body recover before they administered general anaesthesia again. It was possible that my body could develop a tolerance towards general anaesthesia, leading to complications in my future surgeries. Ria did some research and realized this was true.

The reason I go into detail about this decision is because of a terrible turn of events that took place sometime later. After the success of the campaign, Dr Jain invited me to his clinic. I assumed it was going to be a follow-up on my post-operative recovery process.

I was ceremoniously ushered into his office on the day of my visit. The lights were dim and I could make out Dr Jain sitting on his chair. He asked me to sit on the stool placed just across from him.

I sat down, feeling terrified – despite my newfound success and confidence – of this doctor that the whole world admired and revered. Here he was, a formidable Padma Shri winner, and when he said sit, I sat.

Placing his phone on a tripod on his table, with its camera angled towards me, he said: 'Now, repeat the words you said in your beauty tutorial videos. Say the exact words, but try to look sad.' For a minute I looked into the camera in shock. I didn't understand what was going on. Why? Why did he think it would be okay to ask for such an odd recital, and, more importantly, why did he want to record it? I wondered if it was for his personal YouTube channel that offered numerous other heart-breaking videos of survivors.

I stumbled through my lines, terrified. Once he was done recording, he simply flicked on the lights and told me to leave. He never asked me how I was doing, neither did he discuss the next steps towards further recovery. I left, feeling uneasy and scared. I called Ria. She laughed when she heard what had happened. As it turns out, Dr Jain had called her and demanded he be mentioned in the credits for all the Beauty Tips for Reshma videos, even though he had nothing to do with the campaign. Something seemed wrong. No critically acclaimed doctor and an accomplished grown man should be sitting in a dark room, desperately seeking credit for every small accomplishment that was made in his periphery. It was sad to see that someone so revered by the public was in real life petty, crude, uncompassionate and insecure. The man he turned out to be was at odds with how the world viewed him. I wonder how many secrets public figures harbour in their private lives. I was very disturbed that day. I still feel queasy when I remember that dark room with the small phone camera flash beaming at my confused, reluctant face.

The more I interacted with Dr Jain, the more I realized that his sole purpose lay in winning accolades and boosting his public image. A few times over the year he treated me, numerous documentary channels had reached out to Make Love Not Scars to shoot my story and recovery process. Dr Jain would reschedule my surgeries to accommodate the filming of these documentaries since he wanted to showcase his surgical talent on camera and he had found the perfect guinea pig. One day, on 25 January 2016, a globally recognized television channel reached out to Make Love Not Scars, expressing their intention to shoot a short feature film on me. Ria thought it would be great to have Dr Jain on board as well. We emailed him and he, of course, agreed. In February, the producers and directors flew in from London for the shoot.

Dr Jain's office called me one day to tell me I was scheduled for surgery on 27 February. I was shocked. I had barely recovered from my last procedure, and from what I could recall, I was not to go in for surgery for another few months. I shared my deep misgivings with Ria.

Ria wrote to Dr Jain saying that we all agreed that only my consultation with him should be shot on 26 February. He never responded and we thought there had been some miscommunication.

On 26 February, I went to Dr Jain's clinic for my consultation and shoot. The friendly documentary crew had already arrived. While I could not speak with the foreigners, the Indian members of the crew made me feel like I was one of them. We went into Dr Jain's office for my consultation, but before the crew could ask where to set up their equipment, Dr Jain handed me an 'admit card'. 'If you shoot, it will only be when I'm operating on her. She's due for surgery at Bombay Hospital at 6 p.m. today so there's no need to set up here.'

I looked at the crew in shock. Why was he handing me an admit card with a patient ID for the hospital? 'Sir,' said a female producer who I had spoken to the most over the last few days as they shot their film. 'We were not aware of this. Hadn't you said earlier that it is dangerous for Reshma to go in for surgery anytime soon? We don't have to shoot a live surgery; it may be best to proceed as planned.'

'Absolutely not,' he said. Then he turned to me: 'Reshma, your surgery is at 6 p.m. today and they will shoot it.'

Confused, unsettled, the crew and I walked out of the room. The producer called Ria in a panic, as I started to feel very afraid. Not only was I not prepared emotionally, I felt like Dr Jain's tool, his means to glory. Also, every other time I was to go in for surgery, I had been instructed to not eat for twelve hours prior. This time, however, I received no such instruction. I had been drinking water and tea and had eaten a heavy breakfast. I wondered if Dr Jain would have treated one of his wealthier, more powerful patients the same way he was treating me. The producer handed me a phone. It was Ria. 'I don't want this surgery,' I said, my eyes welling up. 'I'm not ready.'

'I know,' said Ria. 'Don't worry, just walk away. I can't believe this man. This surgery is dangerous for you. With the number of times you've been under general anaesthesia recently, it's not okay for you to go through it again so soon. He had himself said that you would need to wait for another six months!'

Meanwhile, the producer had gone back into Dr Jain's office to knock some sense into him. I heard loud voices before she came back out. 'He's firm that Reshma will have her surgery today.'

We spoke to Ria again. 'Just walk out. Walk out before he forces you into something you are not willing to go through. I will find you a better doctor and I'm so sorry about this.'

With that, the producers and I left Dr Jain's office. That was, for me, the last straw. The fact that my doctor had put his own career before my health outraged me. He was vengeful and cruel. As a result of my decision that day, he set out to ruin me as well as Make Love Not Scars. Even today, we are fighting his false allegations against us. He is yet to return the money Make Love Not Scars had deposited to the hospital for my surgeries that were never performed. My brother Aizaz and I visited the hospital numerous times, only to be told that the funds could not be given to me without Dr Jain's authorization. He never picked up our calls or responded to emails. The only way forward was the legal route. I am still baffled by men like him.

While my journey has had and will continue to have dark moments, I am thankful that it has, for the most part, been beautiful, honest, victorious.

17

New York Fashion Week

NOW THAT I WAS no longer being treated by Dr Jain, I told Ria I did not wish to have any more surgeries for some time. We stopped meeting doctors and I began to focus my energy on representing Make Love Not Scars. Between April 2016 and September 2016, an important collaboration started to take shape between Make Love Not Scars, FTL Moda and myself.

While Make Love Not Scars operated out of New Delhi, I lived in Mumbai. Ria spends her time between these two cities. One day, towards the beginning of August 2016, Ria called and asked me to go over to her mother Kate Kayani's apartment. It was more of an order, to be honest: 'Come over now! No excuses.'

Ria's mother Kate (who I call Kate Aunty) works in Mumbai and her home is like our second home. The doors are always open to all of Ria's friends and the members of Make Love Not Scars. There have been months when Ria and Tania practically forgot that they also have homes in Delhi, as the three of us made ourselves comfortable in Kate Aunty's apartment, discussing our next big plan for weeks and numerous buckets of KFC.

I entered Kate Aunty's house and dropped my bag on the couch. Ria had her laptop open and was sitting on the dining table. 'Come, sit here,' she said, patting the empty chair next to hers. 'Do you want anything to drink?'

'Nah,' I said as I sat down.

'Mom, let's get her water anyway,' said Ria. Kate Aunty brought me a glass of water.

Ria handed Kate Aunty her phone. 'I'm going to show you something, and Mom's going to record your reaction, okay?'

'What? Why?' I asked, excitedly. 'Did you buy me a present?'

Ria and Kate Aunty burst out laughing. 'You'll see. Pay attention to the screen now.' I turned my eyes to the screen, also wondering if the two ladies were playing a prank on me as they sometimes do.

Ria typed something on Google and a bunch of images came up. 'Reshma, do you know where this is?' I stared at beautiful, stunning aerial shots of skyscrapers. I shook my head.

'Nothing comes to mind?'

I didn't really know much about the world outside my home; just that some of my father's friends had previously migrated to the Middle East for blue-collar jobs. Whenever they spoke of those Gulf countries, they would tell us about beautiful clean roads and tall, glittering buildings. I took the first and only name that came to mind. 'Dubai ...?'

'Guess again,' said Ria.

I stared at the screen, biting my lip, but could think of nothing else. That's how little I knew of the world outside Mumbai. At last, I named a second place, one which we all believed to be heaven on earth. 'America?' Everyone knew that no one was poor in America, nothing was scarce, and that everybody lived, studied, and married out of their own choice. We had watched many Hollywood movies dubbed in Hindi on local TV channels.

'Okaaay!' said Ria excitedly. I looked up at Kate Aunty with pride. I had passed the test!

I continued to stare at the skyscrapers. 'Get this,' said Ria. 'There's a very big fashion show that takes place in New York, the place I just showed you.'

'Hmm,' I muttered, wondering what this had to do with me.

'So ... in September,' she continued, her voice rising an octave higher with every word spoken, 'you will be going to America and walking on this show!'

My heart began to race the minute I heard her say I would be going to America! In fact, I had guessed the end of her sentence before she had finished it, because of how her voice was dripping with excitement. I looked away from the screen, smiling at Kate Aunty, at Ria, at nothing. It didn't make sense to me. How could I be going to New York!

I was laughing and crying. Once again, I had lost my words. 'Really!' said Ria. 'It's true! Are you excited?' Of course I was. Excitement and disbelief coursed through my veins and I hid my face in my hands, not wanting Ria or Kate Aunty to see me cry. I was in shock. Never in my life had I dreamt of seeing another country, and to be told that I would be going to New York to walk the runway at a fashion show was at odds with even my wildest dreams.

Children in my chawl would all dream of going to America and driving taxis. That was what the US meant to us. From where I came, America was a far-fetched dream, a name whispered only with reverence. I realized I would be the first person among my family and friends to go to America. I would probably be one of the first to even apply for a passport! Abba and Ammi would be so proud. I was going from one of the smallest chawls in India to one of the largest cities in the world. I couldn't wait to tell them. 'Are you nervous?' asked Ria, repeatedly. 'Are you excited that you will walk down this big ramp with some of the world's most famous models?' I continued to cry. 'I feel really good,' I said through my tears. Everyone laughed.

We talked about New York for over two hours. I had to know the whole story. I needed to know why I had been chosen when there were millions of other girls like me, all of whom deserved the same chance. 'Because you showed up when no one did, Reshma,' Ria said to me. 'You were there for every shoot, every interview, and every project even though people thought it would lead to nothing.'

Thanks to the success of the #endacidsale campaign, the world was rapidly learning more about acid attacks through my story. On 20 April 2016, Ria received an email from FTL Moda, a multipurpose firm that specializes in providing services to large fashion labels. They were producing a fashion show for New York Fashion Week 2016 and had previously curated renowned shows for designers focusing on inclusivity and diversity. They wanted to collaborate with Make Love Not Scars and wanted me to walk the ramp for designer Archana Kochhar's label. It would be fitting for me to represent an Indian designer on an international platform, they said. I asked Ria why she hadn't told me earlier. 'I wanted the deal to be finalized; I didn't want to see you disappointed in case it fell through. FTL Moda and Make Love Not Scars signed the final contracts today. It's only missing your signature.' I signed without a second thought.

'You need to apply for a passport!' Ria was back to panic mode as she called my brother Aizaz to give him the good news. Aizaz would know how to go about the paperwork. I could hear him asking Ria over and over again if this was a joke. When Ria and I finally convinced him that I had, in fact, been invited to walk for New York Fashion Week, he suddenly had to go. 'I have to go tell everyone – let me call you back!!'

Although I was still very excited, I had also begun to feel a little anxious. 'Will I have to go alone? I don't speak English. What about the flights? What if they deny my visa?'

My dreams were coming true, but they could also be broken very easily. 'Don't worry,' said Ria. 'FTL Moda will be buying your flight tickets and paying for your hotel, and I will go with you. Dad's a pilot, remember!' I laughed, feeling relieved.

Aizaz called back after some time. 'I've made a list of everything we need to apply for Reshma's passport. And she doesn't even have a birth certificate.'

'What?' screeched Ria. 'How? How does she not have a birth certificate?'

As it turns out, many people in India don't have birth certificates. So many parents are simply oblivious to the importance of this document. Owing to this ignorance, the Government of India has put processes in place that allow one to apply for a birth certificate at any point during the length of their life. I had to go to Allahabad to apply for mine. In order to prove the approximate year of my birth, I needed to attach a school-leaving certificate from the school I last attended, which happened to be in Mau Aima, in Allahabad district.

Ria spoke to FTL Moda and confirmed that I was ready to go to New York and that we were working on getting all my paperwork in order to apply for a passport and an emergency US visa. It was already August, and we were set to fly to New York on 6 September.

During the first week of August, Ria contacted everyone she knew to help me with my paperwork. Aizaz and I flew to Allahabad, where we had trouble applying for a birth certificate. Every time we took our papers to the magistrate, he would deny our request, saying that some document or the other was missing. Perhaps they were hoping for a bribe. At last, one of Ria's friends put us in touch with a local politician in Allahabad, which sped up the process. Some things never change, am I right?

Soon, we applied for an emergency passport under the Tatkal scheme. I then flew to Mumbai for my US visa appointment. I had never flown out of the nation, and we were afraid that the American Embassy would deny my visa application. But I was pleasantly surprised to find that the interviewer had watched my videos before. He granted me a ten-year multiple-entry visa. All my fears and doubts disappeared. There was nothing stopping me from going to New York and I finally came to grips with the grand scale of events of which I would soon be a part.

'I'll be going a couple of days before you,' said Ria. 'I will brief you about everything and will be there to pick you up when you land.'

On the night before I was to fly to New York, Ria sent across numerous scanned notes to Aizaz via email. These notes were written in English and I was to show them to any person at the airport whenever I felt lost. The notes mentioned that I only spoke Hindi and Urdu; they contained my name, flight number, route, purpose of visit, the fact that I had a layover in London, and that I was an acid-attack survivor and needed all the help I could get. I made photocopies and kept them carefully in my bag.

Ammi, Abba, Aizaz, Gulshan, Nargis, and Riyaz, all came to see me off at the airport. Ammi cried tears of happiness. '*Kismat kaisi cheez hoti hai*,' she said, commenting on my destiny. How things had changed. The biggest reason for my happiness, though, was that I hadn't succeeded in taking my own life after the attack. Now here I was, one acid attack and a few suicide attempts later, happier than I had ever been in my life, and this astonished me. At one point I believed I would never speak to anyone again, and yet, I was about to fly to another continent at the other end of the world, all by myself. I couldn't wrap my head around this fact.

I entered the international airport, clutching my passport tight. I checked in and was guided through immigration. My flight was, for the most part, uneventful. This was the first time I had been on a plane with a television screen. It fascinated me and an airhostess showed me how I could watch a movie. I didn't even know where the sockets for the earplugs were! When we landed in London, a member of the ground crew escorted me to my departure gate.

The next leg of the journey was long. Since the time I left my home, boarded another flight in London, and landed in New York, more than twenty-four hours would have passed. I had no idea what to expect by the time the plane touched down in New York. I was so very tired that I wasn't even feeling excited. I longed for some familiarity and rest. I got off the plane and followed the crowd. We walked up to some machines, where I saw people standing and scanning their passports. I tried to do the same with mine, but it didn't work. There were questions on the screen, all in English. I didn't know what to do and looked around for help, but couldn't catch anyone's attention. I stood around, passport in hand, confused and worried.

Ten minutes later a big, burly officer came towards me. He was taller than any man I had seen before and I realized that most people here would be towering over me. 'Reshma Qureshi?' he asked and gestured for me to follow him. He smiled at me and asked some questions. I said 'okay, okay, okay' to everything. I had no idea what he was saying and even simple English words that I previously understood were sounded alien because of the American accent.

We reached a private room. The man took my passport and the notes Ria had handed over to me. I started to feel scared again. I had heard that America had instated serious immigration policies since 9/11 and that Muslims were often questioned separately and sometimes even denied entry into the country. Even Shah Rukh Khan had been stopped at an American airport! I began to cry. Would I be sent back after coming such a long way? Would they put me in prison? I wouldn't be able to call my parents. Did Ria know where I was?

The officer looked at me in shock. 'No, no,' he said repeatedly. He said a lot of things; I registered the words 'stop', 'cry', 'no', 'Reshma'. He then quickly stamped my passport and gestured at me to follow him again. 'Ria, Ria Sharma?' he said to me. I stopped, looked at him, and nodded. He smiled and I smiled back. I understood now. Ria must have asked this kind officer to keep an eye out for me. He guided me through baggage claim and walked me out to an area milling with people. I spotted Ria and ran towards her, all teary and nervous. She hugged me and laughed. She took my luggage from the officer, thanked him profusely, gave him her business card, and we left.

'The officers here don't have to follow a policy of helping passengers, but when I told him your story, he almost cried! He said he would personally bring you over to me,' said Ria. 'I hope you didn't get scared.'

This was the first time I had ever witnessed such incredible kindness from a figure of authority. I was supposed to be in New York for around a week, and in that week, I was repeatedly surprised to find such immense kindness in people. From the moment I landed here, I began to notice how much people smiled, even at total strangers. This was highly refreshing. I felt normal, and more importantly, I felt attractive.

We left the airport and got into a car that smelled like lavenders. The leather seats were so cosy. I fell in love with the local taxis. The roads were clean and there was little traffic. Ria laughed and said that the cab drivers believed this to be traffic. 'Tell them to come to India,' I said. I started to miss my family. I know they would have loved to see New York.

We reached the Carlton Hotel where we were going to stay in one of the suites. Ria had already checked in for both of us. As we rode up the elevator, I was stunned by the lavish, luxurious interiors. I entered my suite and gasped. The large windows overlooked the city of New York. I could see people, all kinds of people, walking faster than I had ever seen people walk in Mumbai. The buildings sparkled under the sun. I was too tired to eat and we fell asleep.

I was supposed to be in New York until 12 September. Ria had told me that a documentary crew would be following us around through my entire stay.

The next morning, we woke up early. The documentary crew arrived at the suite and Ria introduced me to everyone. The crew had members from Europe and America. The director, Livia Alcalde, was renowned for her beautiful imagery, and had won numerous awards at the Global Music Awards, the European Film Festival, the International Film Festival, among others, and the Director of Photography, Greg Harriott, was an Emmy Award-winning cinematographer. The team was also graced by the brilliant assistant director Alejandro Cortés, and the incredibly efficient producer Chiara Nardone. Ria had also invited a friend, Anaaya Udhas, to help us during the next few days.

I was jet-lagged, but we did not have a moment to spare. The fashion show was to take place on 8 September 2016.

Pre-show appointments for interviews were lined up all through 7 September. The documentary crew filmed me getting dressed for B-rolls and took some interviews until around lunchtime. After lunch, we set up for pre-show interviews with the media. The schedule was intense. I had an interview with Reuters at 3:30 p.m., TVE Spain at 5:30, CBS at 6, *Daily Telegraph* at 6:30, the *Independent* at 7, *Lela* at 7:30, *Time* at 8, and *Elle* at 8:30 p.m. Ria acted as my translator, and by the end of the day we were both exhausted and fell into a deep sleep. I don't think I ate anything except for some fruits the whole day.

The following morning, I woke up around 7. I was on edge, bursts of anxiety resulting in shaking hands and restless toes. What I am about to say probably won't make sense to some of my readers, but that morning I almost feared what lay ahead. I knew walking the runway was not just simply that, it wasn't just about fashion; it was the beginning of a global mission to change how certain people were perceived. Today wasn't simply about a statement on acid attacks; we were going to redefine how people should be judged. I already knew that parts of the media would sensationalize the walk and that the real battle was only just beginning. An acid attack in itself is vicious, but what follows is a toxic barrage of stereotypes, pity, and discrimination.

The documentary crew met us again at our suite in the morning. Ria and I made our way to the venue along with them. We stepped into the green room and Ria and I looked at each other, stunned. Extreme stress was flying all around. Each model was being attended to by at least four hair and make-up professionals, organizers were barking orders into cell phones and walkie-talkies, photographers, videographers, and journalists were recording every minute of every activity, and while we were busy assessing the stress of the situation, my documentary team had already set up their cameras and were recording my reactions! I had never seen such busy people in my life, not even in hospitals!

Things were moving faster than I could breathe. Many people believe that fashion is superficial, but in my experience, it is one of the most cut-throat, competitive, and dynamic industries to be in. I was shown to a chair. A producer went up to Ria and gave her quick instructions before walking away. 'You will be trying on a few outfits to see which one fits you best. There will be two shows. One in a few hours, and one in the evening. You will have to get your hair and make-up done after the outfit is finalized. I've told them to be careful with your face and eyes. Interviews between shows and during hair and make-up as well.'

'When will I breathe?' I asked. Ria laughed loudly and translated my joke to everyone present. No one else seemed to find it funny and Ria and I exchanged embarrassed, amused expressions. I was shown to a changing room where I tried on three outfits. At last, I was given a beautiful white fish-cut, floor-length gown with full sleeves and intricate embroidery. I had never worn anything this beautiful before. I then made my way towards the hair and make-up section. Photographers kept flocking in my direction, hoping to capture a striking image of the world's first acid-attack survivor to walk the New York Fashion Week. Which they did. One of these photos later made its way to the cover of *Newsweek* magazine in the Middle East.

As I was getting my hair and make-up done, I was thrilled to see Sunny Leone opposite me, also getting ready for the show! She was to walk the ramp *with me*! At some point, she walked over to say hi. I was so nervous I could barely greet her back. She hugged me and called me an inspiration. This was the first time someone I admired had called me an inspiration. I hugged her right back. She is an open book, warm and friendly, and I felt so comfortable around her.

A few months later I would meet my idol, Shah Rukh Khan, along with Ria, Tania, and some other survivors: Basanti, Mamta, and Sapna. He, too, called me an inspiration. From watching the people I admired on television screens, I had come to stand next to them, brush shoulders with them. Destiny is bittersweet, cruel and kind; it leaves you no clues about the path that you will one day take with effortless ease. You figure it out on your own, and later, you can look back and connect the dots, but in our present moment, who can tell what destiny has in store for us?

I had never walked the runway before, and for fifteen minutes, a choreographer guided me down the ramp and taught me how to pace my walk, when to stop and turn, and where to stop for good photographs. Fifteen minutes was hardly anything and I felt nervous. Soon, we were all asked to remain quiet backstage as the show had finally started. Music was pumping through the doors, the models were all standing in order, and I continued to hold Ria's hand. 'Don't worry,' she whispered. 'I'll be standing on the other side when you exit.'

It was my turn. The choreographer gave me the green light to start moving. My heart was pounding, but there was no time to stop and think. I took a deep breath, remembered why I was there, and stepped up on the ramp.

It was over before it started. All that nervousness faded away and was replaced with flashing lights, thunderous applause, and a deep sense of pride and fulfilment. I got off the stage, my eyes fixed on Ria. We hugged. We didn't say a word to each other but we both knew that the real battle had just started.

#TakeBeautyBack was now trending on Twitter, and the next morning I woke up to find my face splashed across the *New York Times* and the *New York Post*. Ria immediately went online and the documentary crew filmed my reaction as we gauged the magnitude of the coverage. *Time* magazine reported: 'This was not Qureshi's first time standing up as a survivor of acid attacks. She has been making beauty-advice videos on YouTube, which last year doubled as a public-service announcement for an effort in India to stop acid from being available for sale in the open market.'

My debut at the New York Fashion Week made headlines across the globe and was reported extensively by the BBC, *Cosmopolitan*, the *Guardian*, *Hindustan Times*, the *Times of India*, *Daily News*, *India Today*, *Buzzfeed*, *Elle*, the *Daily Telegraph*, *People*, and many more. Once again, we had triggered a global conversation, only this time we were not targeting the government so laws could be amended and enforced; we were speaking to the masses and demanding acceptance, to be treated just like everyone else.

18

Miles to Go before We Sleep

NEW YORK WAS MAGNIFICENT. My trip was short, but I can never forget the city. It was always bright and awake, and safer than most places in India. The next three days after the fashion show were spent filming B-rolls for my documentary. I walked around the city for hours, from the urban jungle of Central Park into the dazzling lights of Times Square. How could one city have such an incredible variety of life? People of all colours, dressed in an array of interesting attires, inhabiting a city that never ceased to captivate me. I learnt what it meant for a city to have character. Artists performed everywhere, some with talents I had never thought possible.

I wanted to make sure I could convey my memories to my friends back in my chawl without losing anything in translation. A melancholy swept over me. I wished they could see what I was seeing. I was jealous of how beautiful everything was. Why couldn't we have such peace, serenity, and purpose in our cities? The city wasn't quiet, but even at its busiest it seemed at ease. There was no aggression in the air. The smiling faces, the unprecedented empathy, the warm welcome that was extended to me by the people of New York will always bring a smile to my face.

I came back to India on 12 September 2016 and the first thing that struck me like a slap across my face were the hostile stares. In New York, people smiled at me. Here, I had to cover my face to avoid people who made me uneasy. A few days after my return to Mumbai I flew to New Delhi for a magazine photoshoot. This was the first time I would meet the CEO of Make Love Not Scars, Tania Singh. While Tania had joined the team just a few days before the launch of the #endacidsale campaign (when she was still studying at Singapore Management University), we had never met because of our varying schedules. She had just returned from Malaysia and dropped by to meet me at the shoot. 'You must stay at my place!' she insisted. We stayed up that whole night, talking about the changes we wished to make in our country.

She asked me what I thought was the biggest difference between New York and India. 'Well,' I said,

'Mumbai is a little more liberal, but Delhi scares me. I saw women walking around at all hours in New York, wearing whatever they wanted, without fear, but the minute I arrive in Delhi, I begin to feel so scared.' Tania agreed: 'For a country that claims to be one of the strongest-moving economies, we are perhaps the weakest when it comes to women's rights.'

That year, in November, the MBC Networks invited Tania and me to Lebanon to be on a television show called *Kalam Nawaem*, one of the highest-rated, female-hosted talk show in the Arab world that focuses on human rights success stories from across the world. It was the first global satellite-broadcasting network in the Middle East and its reach is, beyond doubt, massive.

The show had previously interviewed a whole host of distinguished people who have been making history. Hillary Clinton (the 67th United States Secretary of State), Rania Al-Abdullah (the Queen Consort of Jordan), Amina J. Mohammed (the fifth Deputy Secretary-General of the United Nations), Salma Hayek (the renowned Mexican-American film actress), Malala Yousafzai (the youngest Nobel laureate in the world), Will Smith (popular Hollywood actor), and many others of their stature. I cried out of excitement and pride.

We landed in Beirut on 3 November. We had a layover in Doha, and since we were travelling together, Tania and I had a lot of time to talk about the past and the coming years, about the purpose of the New York Fashion Week, and the implications of making my story echo in every corner of the world. The New York Fashion Week had been a happy milestone in my journey and that of Make Love Not Scars, but Ria and I knew that that this was also the start of a radical new battle, the real battle no one was talking about, the battle yet to be won. While we needed to end acid sale, we also needed to change the way people viewed acid-attack survivors. Most of our struggles started after the attack, brought on by the way people treat us.

While we were in Lebanon, Tania met with a kind diplomat from the Indian Embassy. He was pained by my story, but believed the New York Fashion Week was pointless, that it would hardly make a difference. Journalists had been calling Ria, asking her to comment on my photos with Sunny Leone, if it had been a publicity stunt to raise more funds for Make Love Not Scars. Some believed such publicity was compromising the seriousness of acid attacks. Many wondered if survivors were being objectified, while others speculated that big corporate houses were using me to raise their PR image. But Ria and Tania would laugh these questions away. Such allegations were absurd, but they still hurt on a deeper level because it meant our message wasn't reaching the public properly. Us survivors wish to be treated the same as anyone else, and as long as such questions are being raised, our work isn't over. Acid-attack survivors will truly be accepted into society the day our faces are not blurred by television channels because they are 'graphic', or when we can walk down a fashion ramp *without* making global headlines.

Tania, Ria, and I have been on numerous television shows and given hundreds of interviews, yet the most common question hurled at us is: 'What's the point?'

The point is that acid-attack survivors in India are shamed. We live in a culture of victim-blaming. Many of us never leave our homes because of the hostile stares, gestures, comments directed at us, and because of how differently we are treated from everyone else. Only a handful of us ever find jobs and even if some of us do, it is in government-sanctioned projects that require us to be hired under quotas.

As for those television journalists who called me inspiring yet blurred my face, I ask them to look within and realize how counterproductive they have been to my cause. Rather than accepting me for who I am, they have reinforced that I have a face I should be hiding. Well, I cannot change my face. Our potential employers say that there is nothing they want more than to propagate inclusivity, yet inform us later that we can't be in customer-facing roles. Rather than standing up for inclusivity, they make us believe we should be ashamed of coming out in public. Such people are hypocrites.

As long as discrimination like this is rampant, I will continue to tell my story and break barriers. Many believe that my unparalleled success at the New York Fashion Week was a historical moment for acid-attack survivors. I most certainly hope so, because never again in the history of the world would I wish for a story like that to make global headlines. How often do you flip through the pages of the newspaper to find headlines going: 'Nineteen-year-old Girl Walks the New York Fashion Week'? Almost never, because it is now normal, accepted. I wish that acid-attack survivors will be accepted by society, that our presence outside hospitals, classrooms, courtrooms, and bedrooms will be seen as normal, or, if not, at least normal enough to not make headlines.

We appreciate the global conversations our projects and movements trigger. Without awareness, we would remain unsuccessful. While many still believe our statements are pointless, we know from first-hand experience that we are effecting actual change at the grassroots level. After our success with #endacidsale, a corporate funder funded a dream project for Make Love Not Scars to produce a documentary on acid attacks. After our success at the New York Fashion Week, Akshay Taneja, of Rent A Closet and the TDI Group, reached out to us to collaborate for a charity fashion show. India's leading designers, the likes of Archana

Kochhar, Ranna Gill, Rohit Bal, Anita Dongre, and Varun Bahl, readily agreed to donate their outfits for auction. The proceeds would go towards the benefit and rehabilitation of acid-attack survivors. The question was: how would we throw a fashion show of such magnitude without any resources? Thankfully, Ria and Tania knew Mr Keshav Suri, Executive Director of the Lalit Suri Hospitality Group, and he was touched by our story. They agreed to host the show and also raised funds for a survivor's surgery. We hosted the fashion show on 25 November 2017 at Kitty Su at The LaLiT, Barakhamba Road, and the hotel bore all the costs. The incredible General Manager, Mr Vivek Shuka, personally ensured that the event went off as smoothly as possible. Keshav Suri handpicked the food and drinks, and the chef and his team worked tirelessly. We made headlines yet again. What touched us most deeply, however, was that their team personally helped us organize the event. They provided the resources, the space, entertainment, and, most importantly, their time. Running a hotel as large as The LaLiT is time-intensive, and the fact that the key managers and executive director personally invested their precious time to our campaign was extremely heart-warming.

People opened their doors and their hearts to our cause. For the longest time, private companies were happy to hire acid-attack survivors, but never in customer-facing roles. However, a handful of trailblazers, such as Aradhana Lal from the Lemon Tree Hotels and Keshav Suri from the Lalit Suri Hospitality Group, are working tirelessly to end discrimination at the workplace. I, along with another survivor, Meena, now intern in the hospitality department of the LaLiT Hotel and Mr Suri proudly announced that every role for us in the hotel would be a customer-facing role. 'I don't want you or anyone to be hidden away,' he said to us, aghast at some of our past experiences. 'I want the survivors to be at our front desks, to be heard and seen, and if anyone has a problem with that, they don't have to come to our hotels. Why should you be ashamed? It is the world that should be ashamed of what it did to you.' A wonderful man, Mr Suri has stood by minorities in ways no one ever has before. He is today openly working towards changing laws that criminalize the LGBTQ+ community. Very recently, a big battle was won on that front. Similarly, Ms Lal is single-handedly managing the CSR of over forty-five Lemon Tree hotels across India. She is training her differently abled employees to work at their hotels and has offered mentorship and guidance to the Make Love Not Scars team as well.

Because of our voice, powerful people with noble ideals have joined our cause. So, yes, there is a point to every single campaign we roll out, there is a point to every 'useless' fashion show and every single 'publicity stunt'. All of these efforts have led to actual, tangible change.

My journey has been long, hard, humbling, exciting. Along this journey, I've learnt that change is gradual. Plans change and doors open and close, and all we have to do is seize every opportunity.

I often wonder what the purpose of life is. When Tania and I were in Lebanon, we met some of her local friends, who showed us some of the horrors of the Syrian War. Lebanon had just elected their first president in over two years, and while the nation was celebrating, twenty-five per cent of the population was mourning the loss of loved ones across the border. Around a quarter of the country's population comprises refugees. We saw many injured children and frail, old people begging on street corners, weeping mothers with outstretched hands. Tania and I felt saddened by our helplessness. We went out for dinner that night, and I knew Tania wished she could help the refugees instead. I told her something that I had heard a long time ago. The problems we face are often unimaginably difficult just as our capacities are limited. We need to work with what we have at hand, and before we know it we will have accomplished something we never imagined possible. I've learnt that it is the small changes that ultimately lead to the big ones, and that is the truth I now live by.

All I did after my attack was survive. And that made all the difference. If I had succeeded in killing myself, you would not be holding this book in your hands. The #endacidsale campaign would never have taken off, I would never have walked the New York Fashion Week, and Make Love Not Scars would probably be going in another direction altogether. I tell everyone my story because it makes a difference, and I intend to keep making a difference. I hope you will too.

Epilogue

MY JOURNEY IS NOT mine alone. I never believed in destiny, but now the word gives me comfort. I had lost all faith in this world after my attack. I wanted to die and I blamed the world for its violence. But this same world led me towards people who made it their life's work to help me and many others like me. There are many women who have suffered fates much worse than mine. Some live to tell the tale, while many have succumbed to their destined deaths. I have now made it *my* life's work to speak up for those who can't because I would not want my worst enemy to suffer the way I did. Make Love Not Scars helping me rebuild my life and individuals and corporations giving my voice a platform have also made me realize that I am one of the privileged few. Despite all my sufferings, I am glad I was able to find my voice. God has put me on the path of survival, and I will make the most of it.

I hope this book inspires you to make a change in your own community, because my story is not mine alone, it's for the millions of people who are fighting oppression today. If you are reading it soon after its publication, I am most likely in Beverly Hills for a free prosthetic eye surgery, funded by Face Forward, an organization that provides emotional support and reconstructive surgery for survivors of domestic violence, human trafficking, and other cruel and criminal acts. I was able to find the right medical aid, funded by an international organization that raised funds for my treatment by appealing to kind strangers. That is the power of our world.

Change is slow, gradual. You can be a part of it in your own small way. Donate if you can, a rupee a month if that's all you have, volunteer your time, and, most importantly, spread the word. Be the best version of yourself and the world, I believe, will be a better place.

Afterword

I MET RESHMA, IN MY capacity as Deputy First Minister of Scotland, during a visit to Mumbai in December 2017. I had the pleasure of seeing her taking part in a fashion show that had been arranged to celebrate a partnership between Glasgow Kelvin College in Scotland, Indian educational institutions and the organisation Make Love Not Scars. Speaking to Reshma after the show, I was overwhelmed by what had happened to her and how she had not only survived a devastating acid attack, but had grown into an inspirational young woman with influence on a global stage.

Reading Reshma's story from when she was a young girl to the person she is today presents the reader with a journey of many conflicting emotions. The love of her family is evident, brutally contrasting with the treatment both she and her sister received at the hands of others. The account of the attack itself and subsequent road to recovery is harrowing in the extreme. However, through the agonies of her recovery, a light begins to shine for Reshma and it is evident that a new life is beginning for her.

Her story is extremely relevant in today's world where acid attacks are becoming a global problem. With numbers rising across the world, acid attacks are a problem that must be tackled swiftly and fast. Reshma's memoir highlights the brutal effects of surviving an acid attack and compels one to face the fact that acid attacks are not just a statistic – but a deeply personal struggle faced by thousands.

This is an important book. As well as describing suffering, it is also about hope, about the support of family and friends, about the human spirit and the triumph of love over hate. It is a truly inspirational read.

Edinburgh
September 2018

John Swinney
Deputy First Minister of
Scotland

Acknowledgements

I HAVE WAITED A long time to share my story with the world, and it has finally happened! Thank you to my friend and co-writer, Tania Singh, thanks to my agent, Kanishka Gupta, and thank you, Teesta Guha Sarkar, my editor at Pan Macmillan India, for letting me tell it from the heart. My great wish is that it lends courage to those like myself, and to all my readers and well-wishers.

A gigantic thank you and many hugs to my rock, Ria Sharma, and to Abba, Ammi, Aizaz, Gulshan, Nargis, Riyaz, and everyone else who has stood by me along the way.

Reshma Qureshi

Although this book chronicles the journey of one acid-attack survivor, Reshma Qureshi, I would like to acknowledge each and every survivor who has been through an acid attack. As they say, 'A single death is a tragedy, a million deaths is a statistic.' There are thousands of survivors being attacked with acid every year. Some survive, while many succumb to this gruesome crime. I acknowledge each and every one of you and will keep on striving to prevent people from being inflicted with this terrible pain.

Thank you for trusting me with your story, Reshma. Your courage in narrating such an incredible story is truly inspiring.

To my best friend and the founder of Make Love Not Scars, Ria Sharma – I sometimes feel that we were destined to be friends. You've been here for me through every single achievement, every failure, through good times and bad. Your heart is made of gold, and I am so thankful for your friendship.

To my parents and my sister – Ritu, Micky, Seleena. You have been more excited about my milestones than even myself. Thank you for bearing with the odd hours at which I function, my erratic moods and the unending rants. I would not be here without you, and thank you, also, for investing in my dreams. If everyone in the world had families like ours, the world would be a kinder place.

To my dream team, Kanishka Gupta, my agent, and Teesta Guha Sarkar, my editor at Pan Macmillan India – thank you. Your commitment to giving this book the best chance for success is extraordinary. You have made this journey so effortless, and I'm glad this book is touched by your magic.

To my nani, my maasi (Renu), my masad (Gagan), to Aman and Kareena – thank you for being there every step of the way. I was not an easy child or teenager, but I hope I can MAKE you proud in the future. To my grandparents and maasi who aren't here to read this book – I know you would have been proud and I'm thinking of you. Each and every one of you has fed my love for books and stories. I'll always cherish that.

This is also a wonderful occasion to thank Kate Kayani for always giving me a lovely home to crash in when I was working in Mumbai and unwinding in Goa, and to Monica and Raman Sharma for ensuring I was well fed while I lay in your daughter's bed, forcing myself to write. Thank you so much!

Harshik Suraiya and Vinit Bhatt, you've been a part of Reshma's journey before most people even knew her story. Thank you for treating this memoir with so much love.

To my oldest and dearest friends – Ragini, Devika M., Devika K., Shreya and Garima. We've been friends for almost two decades. I value you more than I could ever put into words. Thank you for your invaluable advice along the way.

To my friends from college, the ones I call my second family. I love you all. Kriti and Evelyn, this book would be filled with millions of errors if it wasn't for your careful editing and feedback. Sushant (especially), Adrien, Vasudha, Vishal and Daga – thank you for your unwavering support through this journey. Devika Agarwal, thank you for the days you let me spend holed up in your room, writing away at all weird hours.

To Keshav Suri – your commitment to using your voice to make a difference in the lives of so many people is inspiring. Thank you for supporting Make Love Not Scars and our cause.

To Alastair McGhee, your support in helping us get this story into the right hands has been so generous. Thank you for all the time you invested in our journey. Gary Mainor, your support has been no less heartening.

To all my friends who have helped Make Love Not Scars in their own unique ways. I am so humbled by your support. Akshay Taneja, Umang, LDM, Rohan Shroff, Shivikka, Amar, Ishan, Dhruv, Shivam, Sukanya, Suruchi, Sahaj, Vishnu, Tarini and Kabir, Sanchi Gupta, Jessica, Rohan Wadhwa, Aneesh and Shikhar – you're all rockstars! I remember every investment you made, with your time, energy and resources, and I thank you all so much.

Tania Singh

A Message from the Authors

Dear Reader,

Thank you so much for picking up this copy of *Being Reshma*. Your support is truly humbling. If you have enjoyed the book and would like to contribute towards its success, please do spread the word amongst your friends and family. Please also leave a review on Amazon and Goodreads. It would go a long way!

We would love to hear from you too. You can interact with the authors and the team at Make Love Not Scars here:

Facebook
Reshma Qureshi: @beingreshma
Tania Singh: @itstaniasingh
Make Love Not Scars: @makelovenotscars

Instagram
Reshma Qureshi: @beingreshma
Tania Singh: @itstaniasingh
Make Love Not Scars: @makeluvnotscars

Twitter
Reshma Qureshi: @reshmaqureshi_b
Make Love Not Scars: @makeluvnotscars

Lots of love,
Reshma and Tania
New Delhi, 2019